LIFE IN THE PEARL
Reflections of a not-so-grown up boy

DR. STEVEN A. JIRGAL

To Joshua, Caleb, and Sarah, may you look back with great fondness on your growing-up years. May those memories bring a smile to your face, joy to your soul, and a gentle and satisfying sigh to your heart.

To my parents—John and Reggie Jirgal, for having the foresight in moving to Pearl River which at the time, was just a blip on the map north of the New Jersey border.

And to the class of 1976 for creating enough memories to fill the minds of an army of people.

TABLE OF CONTENTS

INTRODUCTION

Looking back over the generation in which I grew up, it was the proverbial best of times and worst of times.

There were several downturns in our country which could easily have developed into a rather pessimistic view of life in general. We lived through the Viet Nam war and saw so many atrocities brought to us by the media. Watergate instilled in us tremendous doubt regarding those who were our governmental leaders. We were glued to the television as the news broke about the assassinations of Martin Luther King Jr. and President John F. Kennedy. We watched in horror as the details of Charlie Manson and *the family* unfolded. We took notice of the gas lines that ran for miles and tested the patience of young and old alike. Those instances were dark moments that could easily have filled our hearts with anger, fear, and discouragement.

But those days also gave us so much hope! We watched as technological advances brought us everything from push button phones to the Apple computer. No longer were we slaves to the spring-loaded return dial on the phone (which gave our finger a free ride back), and computers that took up an entire classroom wall. We enjoyed going from a world of black and white boxes with rabbit ears decorated with tin foil, to color television and a multitude of channels. Our ears witnessed the recording industry move from reel to reel, to 8 tracks, to cassettes, and finally to CDs.

Through the combination of television and radio, we got to distantly experience the social phenomena of Woodstock which brought us sex, drugs, and rock 'n roll. More advances brought to our ears musical icons such as The Beatles, Led Zeppelin, The Beach Boys, Elvis, Jimi Hendrix, Chicago, Janis Joplin, David Bowie, The Bee Gees, CCR, The Monkees, and Mick Jagger and his Rolling Stones. We were mesmerized as Michael Jackson *moon walked* from the *Jackson 5* to grow into an entertainment icon as a solo artist. We saw music evolve from rock 'n roll to disco, and the beginning of punk rock and rap. We saw giants such as Billy Joel debut with *Piano Man* and went crazy with identification when Bruce Springsteen introduced us to his enduring hit *Born to Run*.

In Sports, we witnessed Cassius Clay change his name (Mohammad Ali) and the face of boxing when he downed Sonny Liston and we saw Billie Jean King silence Bobby Riggs in *The Battle of the Sexes* on the tennis court. Those days gave us The Green Bay Packers defeating the Kansas City Chiefs in the first ever *Super Bowl*, and we celebrated heartily when our own Joe Willie Namath (Broadway Joe) and his Jets defeated the Baltimore Colts in Super Bowl III (16-7). We stared in wonder as Hank Aaron put to rest Babe Ruth's home run record by sending one over the wall for the 715th time.

Entertainment poured from our television sets, and we enjoyed shows like *Happy Days, Charlie's Angels, The Muppets, The Godfather*, and *MASH*. We saw Larry Hagman go from *I Dream of Jeannie* to *Dallas* in a blink. We were held captive both by *Saturday Night Fever* and *Saturday Night Live*. It was during that time that a new wave of horror films emerged, and we cringed while watching Stephen King's *Carrie*. Mad Magazine was the magazine of choice for our young eyes and each edition gave us Alfred E. Newman on the cover.

In 1973 the Twin Towers were erected, and our stomachs were in knots a year later when Philippe Petit (1994) walked a tight rope from one building to the other.

Though *Star Wars* was fantasy, the first man on the moon, Neil Armstrong (1969) was reality and our generation witnessed both events. Armstrong's iconic words, "One small step for man, one giant leap for mankind" still echo in our ears today.

Those were the days when James Bond was the coolest man around, Disneyland was the desired destination of every child, and *Greasy Kids Stuff* kept the long hair of so many teens in place. The

Corvette was the car to covet: Time was whittled away by playing with a slinky, rock 'em sock 'em robots, etch-a-sketch, burning incense, or watching a lava lamp. Our emotions were revealed simply by glancing at the *mood ring* on our finger. *Bell-Bottoms* were the rage with a few pushing the envelope by wearing *Elephant Bells*. If you were lucky enough to have one, you could spend an entire afternoon in front of the television set playing *Pong* and top off the evening with a rousing game of Monopoly.

Yes, those were the days! They were filled with fear and wonder, hope and discouragement. It seemed to be a balance of incredible advances in one area, while deep struggles in another. But all in all, they were great personal days filled with carefree roving and new sights and sounds around every corner. The safety of friends and family was always close at hand and the bright hope of tomorrow was to be embraced by the rising of the next day's sun. And I am so thankful that I grew up in such a good place and at such a good time.

That place is Pearl River, New York. The very name carries a certain ring to it—almost romantic. Originally, the town's name was Middletown but then it was changed to *Muddy Creek*. Tradition holds that later someone found some freshwater mussels in the town creek and opened one to find a pearl, hence the name change.

Pearl River is actually a hamlet of Orangetown with a current population of about 16,000. It's not necessarily a sleepy town or one that time forgot. There have been many changes and improvements over its almost 150 years of existence. It maintains a high school, middle school, several elementary schools, and a Catholic school (St. Margaret's).

As a hamlet, Pearl River is the second largest one in New York State and is nestled in the arms of the town of Orangetown. It was founded in 1872 and carries classic street names such as Main Street, Central Avenue, Washington Avenue, Lincoln Avenue, Middletown Road, Park Avenue, and John Street. This small town carries the nickname "The Town of Friendly People."

-1-
MOM & DAD
(John & Reggie)

I'm thankful that my parents stayed together. We witnessed them fighting hard but loving just as hard. Mom was from Queens and Dad grew up in Chicago. Attending Princeton brought my Dad to the east coast while Mom was enrolled at St. John's University. They met on a blind date. Their roommates were engaged to one another and thought they might be a good fit (they were right). On their first date, they really didn't get along too well and figured their relationship wouldn't go anywhere. But somehow, and thankfully so, they went out again and as they say, the rest is history.

After getting married they moved to Astoria, Queens and went to work. Mom worked as a pharmacist and Dad managed a movie theatre. Mom has the distinction of babysitting for Ronnie Howard—before he became Opie. (His family lived in the apartment below). When John, Jeff, and Dorothy came along it was off to "Upstate New York."

Pearl River is where our family settled in 1956. They migrated from Queens and worked their way up route 9W (The Palisades Parkway wasn't built yet) to begin a life in this small suburb of New York City. The home they built cost just over $14,000 and boasted two bedrooms and one bath as well as a full basement. (Dad added on to that shortly after moving in as our family grew quickly from five to eight.)

Not far to the north lies Bear Mountain and West Point. To the west and south is New Jersey and to the east is the mighty and historic Hudson River and Westchester County. Twenty minutes of traveling southeast brings you to Manhattan Island and all the adventure and entertainment one could ask of a major U.S. city.

Dad was very smart but very firm. He was the compliant type and wanted us to be compliant as well—we didn't do so well in that area. He had a short fuse which seemed to stay lit. He was a problem solver, and very industrious. He held the same job for 38 years in the film industry in New York City and developed a great reputation as one of the best "Grips" in the industry. Back home, he became the Cub Scout Pack Master (pack 137), enriching his enjoyment of the outdoors.

With all the people I've encountered over the years, I still hold that my father was the smartest man I ever met. It seemed he could figure out anything. Early on, in an effort to violate my bedtime, I decided to ask my Dad a question. I knew his explanation would take me past my deadline to be exiled to bed. I don't know why I thought I would end up watching T.V., but it did cross my mind. So, I asked my Dad a question that I was convinced would take a long time to answer and push me past the appointed hour. "Dad, how do planes fly?" The words had barely left my lips when my Dad had out a piece of paper and for the next half-hour explained to me all the key elements of flight. After our session, I went to bed with my head spinning and a strange sense of failure.

When Dad had trouble sleeping you could find him in his chair with a book on his lap. In later years we watched him as he viewed something on television about another country. Shortly after that, he would announce that he was going to the library. He would come back with an armload of books and then announce the inevitable. He was taking a trip. Dad loved to travel and see new things. He was fascinated by other countries and cultures. He loved being immersed in new places with new faces. Before his passing he traveled to not less than 40 different countries. Mom enjoyed travel as well but was not enamored in some of the "off the beaten path" places that Dad enjoyed. She loved Ireland and England and other countries that the general population were more drawn toward. But her heart was always at home.

Dad was a builder and had a shop in the basement. He poured himself into the projects he did around our house. He built two additions onto our home and always seemed to be involved with some home improvement endeavor.

The film industry was a "feast or famine" type of business so he had work that would last for several months followed by long stretches at home. But when he was at home, he would busy himself with projects or be involved with the family in some way. He built our redwood pool (twice), our patio, the garden, the rose trellis, plenty of toys and furniture (dining room table, spoon holder cabinet, garage storage shelves, my brother Casey's bed, the laundry chute, bookshelves, a green house, and several other projects).

Sometimes his home improvement tasks supplied us with stories to share for years. At one point Dad decided to tile the entire main floor bathroom. Next, he took on the job of opening the upstairs staircase. Next on the list was putting down slate in the foyer. After that, it was time to replace the lapboard around the house with siding. But the impact of driving the nails into the back of the house caused the tile in the bathroom to break and come flying off the wall. Back to square one!

Mom was always very creative and loving. She was the consummate housewife. She made our lunches for us every day with almost no exceptions. Along with a dessert of some type and milk money, each of the girls got a sandwich. The boys got one sandwich until middle school and then we each got two sandwiches for the duration of our public schooling. Not long ago, my sister Regina (Winky) and I sat down and added up all the sandwiches Mom made over our years of schooling. We were surprised to find the total eclipsed 19,080 sandwiches.

My mother collected S&H Green stamps. At the check-out counter the cashier would tally up the groceries and dial the amount of stamps your purchase yielded. You could take these stamps home and lick them (we always used a wet washcloth) and put them in your collector's book. When you had enough books, they could be exchanged for prizes. Mom always made a big deal of it and let us help. We would fill a book and then sit on it to make sure it was sealed. By exchanging it we were able to get a badminton set, rubber coated horseshoes, a croquet set, and a set of "Jarts."

I don't know what the manufacturers of the game "Jarts" were thinking when it hit the market. I'm sure that due to injuries sustained it got banned very quickly (and I would not be surprised if the creators of the game spent time in court.) The game basically consisted of two pairs of very heavy dart-like arrows, complete with a semi-pointed end. Two plastic hoops were placed on the ground a certain distance from each other. The object was to toss the "Jart" and try to get it to land in the circle—similar to horseshoes. I don't know if anyone died from getting hit in the head with one of these incoming missiles, but it would not surprise me in the least. Not long ago, I came across a modernized game of "Jarts." The "missiles" were rounded and much smaller with the plastic circles filled with glow-in-the-dark fluid. A wimpy yet surviving generation is sure to follow.

Mom also collected drinking glasses given as a prize for buying dishwashing detergent. Inside each box of detergent was a full-sized glass. We had a complete set for our family of eight with several left over for inevitable breaking.

Along with our drinking glasses, Mom collected "spoon holders." As the name implies, these were decorative crystal pieces that were used to hold spoons. Later, when Mom had a number of these, Dad built her a walnut display case with glass door and a mirrored back. It became the centerpiece of our living room housing some very rare pieces.

She had great joy out of going to antique stores and garage sales. She unashamedly labeled it "Junqing" and to no one's surprise brought home some seriously valuable items. One day she brought home a hall table (which I still have), she purchased for $8. Shortly afterwards its value exceeded $250. A great return on an investment and motivation to continue "Junqing."

Mostly as a joke, but also to send a message, Mom kept a list of all the people she was angry with at that particular point in time. The list was on a large piece of poster board and taped to the back of the basement door. It was her "S" list (use your imagination). If you got on her "S" list, you stayed on it until you did something good or until enough time went by and she deemed it worthy of removal. I think each of us was on that list at one time or another and I'm certain Dad was on it several times.

When something was particularly bothersome to her, she would write what she called *poison pen letters*. A politician, actor, reporter, or school board member often found themselves the target of her frustration as she would take out her pen and communicate her dissatisfaction. This was a one-way communication and Mom never groused over not getting a reply.

Mom always had a story, joke, project, or lesson and she wasn't afraid to laugh at herself. She enjoyed telling the story of the time she went to Wyman-Fisher funeral home on Franklin Avenue to pay respects to a dear friend. Her plan was to go to the visitation and then do some shopping at several stores in town. All through the visitation she kept telling herself, "Hold it together! Hold it together!" Later, when mother was settled in the car the waters flowed. She wiped her tears with a tissue from her coat pocket and did her best to settle down. After a short time, she headed for town. She shopped at the various stores and was perplexed by some of the looks she received. She reasoned that her eyes were probably blood shot and made her way back home. The bathroom mirror revealed the reason behind the strange looks. A pen had exploded in her pocket and the tissue she used was full of black ink. She had smeared the ink all over her face making her look more like a raccoon than a lady.

Nanuet Lake (often called Lake Nanuet) was a place Mom took us on many summer Saturdays. She would pack a big lunch and the entire family would spend the day at the lake. It was very common for us to find the same picnic table each week, and we were normally neighbors with the same people. Mom enjoyed sharing how she was in Mel's Army/Navy store when she heard a man call out, "Hi Reggie!" She looked at him quizzically, so he said, "It's me, John, from the lake." Without thinking my mother hollered back, "Oh, John, I'm sorry. I didn't recognize you with your clothes on!" It takes no imagination to picture the number of heads that turned in her direction that day.

Mom was the glue that held it all together. She had an army of friends and was eager to serve: Den Mother, American Field Service, Booster Club president. She was always one for adventure. The town had a system for directing the volunteer fire fighters to the place of need. Fire alarms were placed on various poles throughout the town. When an alarm was pulled there was a loud horn that blared out the code directing the volunteers to the area. This expedited their arrival.

Mother had the code taped to the wall by the phone. When an alarm went off, she looked up the code to locate the emergency. It wasn't uncommon for her to pile all available kids (sometimes neighboring ones), into the station wagon and speed off to see the fire. It was equally common for Mom to give us a lecture on how that could happen to us if we weren't careful.

In 1972, we all sat with rapt attention when Mom drove us to the hill in front of the middle school. Our treat that afternoon? Watching a helicopter take the crane off the newly completed Uris building (21 stories). What a display of engineering excellence!

Mom had an incredible fear of snakes. Even the ones on T.V. creeped her out and she had to leave the room. Just talking about them made Reggie edgy.

Her great fear of snakes came to a head late one night as she arrived home from a PTA meeting. On the edge of the sidewalk in front of our steps was coiled a large snake blocking her entry into the house. There wasn't enough light to reveal what type it was, she just knew she didn't want any part of it. She went back to the safety of the car to ponder her options.

Not knowing how long the giant serpent would lie there basking in the moonlight eliminated the decision to wait it out. She decided to walk along the street and hustle her way to the back door, hoping the snake didn't have any family members lurking about.

When safely inside, she was miffed to find my father asleep. How could he sleep when her life was in danger? If the snake was indeed poisonous, they would find her body lying on the front steps having died before sunrise.

In the morning she conveyed to Dad her brush with death and suggested that he put out some poison or repellent. Dad walked out the front door and came back moments later requesting that his wife join him.

Reluctantly, my mother went. As she stood next to my grinning Dad, she saw the source of her fear. There on the sidewalk coiled up and ready to strike was a good-sized length of green garden hose.

When the opportunity came, Mom had no trouble telling that story. And if she missed her chance, Dad had no trouble sharing it.

Except for snakes however, Mom loved all animals. We grew up with a plethora of animals around the house. We had the usual pets—dogs and cats, but we also had pets that were outside the norm. We had squirrels, a rabbit, possum, frogs, turtles, an ant farm, chameleons, a parrot, several raccoons, a lizard, and who knows what else.

Mom had a pet squirrel (Nicodemus) that she would feed by hand each night as it came to the back door. She even tossed food to a skunk that would visit. In a fish tank in our garage lived a raccoon that grew to depend on Mom for food.

Mom and Dad each had their way of disciplining us. Dad was extremely quick with his hand while Mom usually used a wooden spoon, belt, or fly swatter. Time out and grounding were methods they both employed with an occasional application of soap-in-the-mouth guaranteeing the eradication of bad language.

Before going on a trip in the trusted station wagon, Dad would line all six of us up and ask each of us if we went to the bathroom. And then he would explain that the tank was full, and we would not be stopping until the tank was empty even if the bladders were full. Next, we all piled in, including Red, our large dog who was a mixture of Irish Setter and Golden Retriever. On more than one occasion, I remember getting a sense that my bladder was not going to cooperate with my Dad's plans, and I sent up a short prayer for a flat tire. We all fought for the very back seat (we did that on buses as well). That seat held two and faced in the opposite direction. That meant that those in the back could make faces at the people in the car behind us.

Car seats were unheard of in those days, and it was common for one of the children to stand in the front seat between Mom and Dad with an arm around each. The back of an arm across the chest served as an "Air bag" and was applied as quickly as the brake.

When going to our grandmother's house in Queens, I would be fascinated by all the traffic and skyscrapers. But what held the biggest fascination was the George Washington Bridge. It seemed to be a million miles above the Hudson and joined the states of New York and New Jersey. My Dad had told us that one time he was involved with a filming project that required him to walk up the massive tubes all the way to the top of the bridge with a camera on his back. To this day, that thought floods my mind when I cross that bridge. The original cost to traverse the bridge was ten cents. This was only to be held until the bridge was paid off. Today, the cost eclipses $17. It is apparent that those in charge could not walk away from the continued revenue.

Each time we drove across the GW, my father would break out in song. He was tone deaf and couldn't carry a tune in a bucket, but that never stopped him from sharing with us in song. He sang his song to the tune of the circus song used in a high wire act. Though it wasn't highly complex, it was highly annoying, and we each prayed he'd forget to sing it—especially when we had friends along. But I'm not sure he ever forgot to sing it. To this day, it is not uncommon for one of his offspring to bust out that song, "George Washington Bridge, the George Washington, Washington Bridge. George Washington Bridge, the George Washington, Washington Bridge." Beyond annoying, I know! But the embarrassment of having friends in the car when this went on was far greater than the annoyance it brought.

When we would drive on the east side of Manhattan (The Harlem River Drive) we would pass a shot tower that is still in place today. During the revolutionary war, a shot tower was invaluable in creating ammunition. Lead was melted in the top room of the tall building. Then it was dropped from the window by the spoonful. The fall would cause the lead to spin and become round. At the base of the tower was a large vat of water. When the lead hit the water, it would cool and harden thus creating a round shot of ammo.

The shot tower is where we decided Mickey Doogan lived. Mickey Doogan was the family ghost. When we drove past, we would roll down our window and call for him to join us in the car. Of course, he always did and stayed with us until we released him on the way home.

My mother's brother, Harry, lived with our grandmother (Mom's Mom). He got into the act by telling us that Micky Doogan ate paper when he was hungry. He would take a piece of paper, attach a string to it, and loop it over the top of the inside of the basement door. The basement of course, was haunted. Then he would slide the paper under the door and onto the kitchen floor. When he called us, we came to watch him feed our family ghost. With our eyes on the paper, he'd pull the string and the paper would shoot under the door. No matter how fast we opened the door we couldn't catch

Micky Doogan escaping. It never occurred to us to look at the inside of the door where the paper was hanging.

Shopping with Mom or Dad was a notable event. Dad didn't take us very often, but when he did, it was all business. We were usually shopping for Mom for Mothers' Day, her birthday, or Christmas. Dad would lecture us before we left the car. We were not to run around, lag, or touch anything. We were hunting for a gift. And like any good hunter, the goal was to "tag it, bag it, and take our trophy home." More than once the back of my head was popped for touching an item as we went by.

Shopping with Mom was a completely different experience. She'd take us to one of her favorite stores, E.J. Korvettes and the adventure would begin. I can't speak factually, but I'm told that while they were serving in Korea, a group of soldiers came up with the idea of joining together to open a large store. They happened to be Jewish and there were eight of them. Thus, the name E.J. Korvettes stood for "Eight Jewish Korean Veterans."

When we entered the store, Mom shared her directives. "Okay. I've got to get some shopping done. Now look at the big clock. When the big hand is on the twelve and the little hand is on the six, you meet me right here. Your father comes home at seven and I have to get dinner ready." And then she would sternly warn us, "And don't you leave the store and don't go with anybody else no matter how nice they look." We all nodded our understanding and affirmation.

Then we were turned loose. Can you imagine what turning six energetic Jirgalettes in E.J. Korvettes looks like? It's a child's dream and an adult shopper's nightmare. Walking was never an option. There was too much to see and too many places to go, and far too many games to play.

A large store is nothing less than a veritable playground when you have a wild imagination. On more than one trip we played hide 'n seek. During one of those games, no one could find my younger brother Casey. He had vanished. We checked the bathroom, behind counters, and even the ladies dressing room (sorry ma'am!). He was just gone. We were about to look for Mom and let her know that our family now only had five children, when I walked past a female manikin with a full-length dress on. Looking down, I noticed she had four feet and two of those feet were donning worn out P.F. Flyers.

The panic was over, and our kid tally was now back to six.

We got in trouble with the manager for zipping Casey up in a winter coat (he was the smallest boy and Winky refused). This was not a big deal except for the fact that the coat was still attached to the circular rack. We were spinning him round and round faster and faster until his legs were sticking almost straight out. He wasn't in any real danger and was laughing the entire time. I suppose the clothes may have been in danger if he vomited but he held his breakfast down. When Mom met us at the door, we were all seated against the wall with a stern warning from the manager. Mom just thought we were simply obeying her orders and only learned about our escapades, years later.

-2-
THE "JIRGALETTES"

Mom and Dad had ideas of having ten kids (on purpose!). But by 1963 the family was rounded out with six children with the energy level and adventurous spirit of twenty.

Generally, you can categorize kids in one of three ways:

Those that are *Rebels*, those that are *Rascals*, and those that are *Regulars* (compliant).

In our family we fell evenly into each of the three categories:

Johnny and Jeff: (the two oldest) *Rebels*

Casey and I: *Rascals*

Dot and Regina: (the girls) *Regulars*

JOHN

John was the oldest and I always looked up to him and learned so much from him. He loved the outdoors and spent his time hunting, trapping, canoeing, and hiking. I went on a couple of hunting trips with him but never bagged anything. Secretly I was satisfied with the failure.

John had a favorite nonsensical poem he enjoyed reciting through the years:

It was a dark and moonlit night,
Two dead boys came out to fight.
Back-to-back they faced each other,
Pulled their knives and shot each other.
A deaf policeman who heard the noise,

Came and arrested the two dead boys.

And if you don't believe this lie is true,
Ask the blind man, he saw it too.
John's favorite riddle was one that couldn't be solved because it involved word play.

Question: You are trapped in a room with no windows and no doors. There is only a mirror and a table. How do you get out?

Answer: Look in the mirror and see what you saw. Take the saw and cut the table in half. Two halves make a hole, and you climb out the hole.

John's military draft number was very low, and he knew he would be called to serve. He was drafted into the army during the Viet Nam war but was released because of a parachuting accident.

I remember Mom picking me up from Little-League and telling me she had to go to Georgia. She told me that John had been in an accident and was hurt badly. I remember her trying to control her emotions and I was somewhat confused about what was going on. I really didn't understand what had happened to John but later learned that the wind had shifted causing him to drift over another jumper's chute. This created a vacuum and his parachute collapsed causing him to fall over 100 feet. His back was broken, and his femur was shattered. He needed extensive surgery and would remain in the hospital for several weeks. He spent the rest of the war recovering and most of the rest of his life in pain.

His love for the outdoors made a natural choice for him to go to Ranger school in Wanakena, New York. While in school, John continued to engage in hunting. One day when he was out with his bow, he came across a black bear. John was startled but settled down in time to get a shot off. His first arrow when through the bears aorta. The bear ran for a half mile thankfully in the opposite direction. When John caught up, he was able to put the bear down with a second shot. He had made our father promise to come up and bring a bear home if he got one. Dad and I left early one morning making the 300-mile trip (one way) to upstate and back in one day. Friends and family and the "Boys Brigade" all got to eat a bowl of bear stew. It could only be described as chewy and the good flavor that it carried was mostly due to the vegetables with which it was cooked.

When he graduated, he started his own tree service. He started small and built the business to earn sustainable income. In the beginning stages his resources included a rope, chainsaw, ladder, and Mom's station wagon. I started working for him when I was thirteen and became his climber (I don't know what my parents were thinking). He got permission to cut dead trees out of some nearby woods and sold firewood from the gleanings. All the wood was split by hand leading to cords of wood, plenty of blisters, and sore muscles.

Later, as his business grew, he added two trucks, more chain saws, a splitter, a chipper, and a sprayer.

To supplement his tree business, he also worked for several years in the film industry as a grip.

JEFF

Jeff was the most mechanical of us all. After high school he worked for a body shop and became an expert on cars. Along with Pearl River High, he attended the Board of Cooperative Education Services (BOCES), and really learned to hone his skills in body mechanics.

Jeff was also the toughest of us all, and never backed down from a fight. He ran with a tough crowd who caused their own version of trouble. In his younger years he built a twin-engine Go-Kart. It had twin two cycle engines with a live axle.

I remember the day the police brought him home because he somehow thought it was acceptable to drive his Go-Kart on the soon-to-be completed route 304. One day Jeff had been driving on the road (his cart topped out at 55mph). The police had been chasing him and he had cut through a couple of yards and around the back of the church. He safely hid his cart in the woods and waited for the heat to die down. He came in the front door acting nonchalant only to find two policemen waiting for him in the kitchen. More trouble for brother Jeff.

He later owned a Camaro which he was particularly proud of. It seemed like he was constantly working on it, doing upgrades and whatever repairs were necessary. One day he was working on the exhaust system. He needed a couple of parts from town, so he jumped in to make the run. On Central Avenue an officer pulled him over. The exchange they had was typical of Jeff:

Officer: "Your muffler's kind of loud don't you think?"
Jeff, pointing to the muffler on the back seat, "It's right there. It's not makin' a sound."
Officer spotting several beer cans on the floor, "And what's with all the beer cans?"
Jeff, thumping the steering wheel, "My grandmother had the car last night. She's such a slob!"
Officer: "Go home kid!"

Jeff was always quick with his mouth most times causing us to cringe at some of the comments he made to Dad.

Dad: "Eat your vegetables!"
Jeff: "I don't want to!"
Dad: "There are children starving in China!"
Jeff: "Yeah? Name two!"

This was predictably followed by a pop on the back of the head.

When Dad would get upset, he'd often pound his fist on the table and scream, "I've had it!"

One day Jeff's response was "Maybe you've had it, but you ain't got it now!"

Another pop to the head followed.

Years later we chided him about having a calcium deposit on the back of his skull.

When Jeff and John were still very young, they came across a large copperhead in the woods. In short order, they killed it with sticks. I still remember seeing the picture in the newspaper of them holding it up. They skinned it and my Dad made a board for its mounting.

Shortly after that, they were on an overnight canoe trip with Dad. While waiting for Dad to return, Jeff was reaching into a pile of floating sticks and tossing them into the river. He pulled on one good sized stick, and it pulled back. He yelled for John to help and the two of them began yanking on the tail of a giant snapping turtle. They fought with the beast and pulled him to land. My Dad came out and in short order they had killed the large creature. When they arrived at home, they enlisted the help of a friend who worked as a butcher and friends and family partook of turtle soup.

Jeff later went to work in the film industry making his own way as a grip.

DOT

Dorothy was number three among the kids. She was Miss Personality in high school becoming the prom queen her junior year. Dot was a majorette, twirling a baton during football games and flaming batons during basketball games. Dot had friends galore and always seemed to be throwing a party at our house. In the basement, on the patio or in the pool, our place was overflowing with Dot's friends.

Back in the day, the drinking age was eighteen. In her senior year, Dorothy and her friends frequently went to different clubs to "dance the night away." Several times she asked me if I wanted to join her and her friends at a Disco joint named *Maximus*. Being underage it was impossible for me to get in. But with the help of a borrowed license, I found myself with big sister dancing with some good-looking older babes and living the dream.

One time when Dot was attending a party in a nearby town, she got ready to leave. A fellow approached her and asked her for her number. She had no interest in him, so she replied, "It's in the phone book." He commented, "But I don't know your last name." As she headed for the door she responded over her shoulder, "That's in the book too!"

When Bill and I started a good-sized fire in St. Aedan's Catholic church (it was under construction), Dot was right there feeding us cardboard, wood, and anything else that would burn. The flames must have been eight feet high explaining the arrival of the police. Through a window, Bill and I made our escape, but Dot didn't run which is why an officer was in our living room a half-hour later.

Most times, Dot was quick to defend all of us. She never was able to defend us physically but with her quick thinking she usually came to our aid verbally. Casey, Billy, and I had set off some fireworks on someone's doorstep—as always, with the motivation of being chased. We got away clean. My parents weren't at home so when the *victims* called our house, they got my sister. She told them to hang on, opened and closed the basement door and informed them that "The boys are still in the basement watching T.V." When we got home, she let us know about the phone call and insisted on having a full run down of what we did.

In high school, like Jeff, Dot attended BOCES and got her practical nursing degree. After high school graduation, she attended Misericordia nursing school (the Bronx), earning her RN. she later earned her bachelor's degree in nursing and worked at Columbia Hospital in Manhattan until retirement from the nursing profession.

CASEY

Three years my junior was my brother Casey. His real name is Thomas James, but everyone called him Casey. He was named after one of Mom's aunts. He was the one that seemed to be loved by everyone and certainly the one that I spent most of my time with. This was undoubtedly due to us being so close in age, and always sharing a room growing up. It seemed like we did everything together.

Casey never seemed to worry. Jeff's explanation was that he didn't have to worry because he really didn't care, and he knew that everyone else would be worrying for him.

Casey always had a great sense of humor and a quick mind. While hanging out in our room one day, Casey spoke up and said, "Hey!" I gave him my attention. He followed with, "Never make fun of the handicapped!" The pause was followed with, "Because if it wasn't for the handicapped, I wouldn't have a place to park!"

I somehow decided that because Casey's bed was closer to the door, it was his job to get me a drink of water each night. One night, Casey decided that this was not *the law of the room*, and he refused. I bugged him relentlessly and finally he capitulated. As I imbibed in my drink of victory he began to laugh. Without much coercion, he let me know that he got the water from the toilet. After I shared it with Mom, she asked, "Casey! What were you thinking?" Without a moment's hesitation Casey said, "I was thinkin' he wasn't gonna ask me for another drink of water."

I'm certain he would be embarrassed for me to share this, but Casey always possessed a generous heart. On more than one occasion, I watched him pull out his wallet to meet the need of someone he came across.

Between riding bikes, fishing, hiking, sailing, and causing more than our share of mischief, Casey and I grew close and remain so to this day.

Casey grew to become an outstanding distance runner. In high school, he was captain of the cross-country team which went on to win the state meet as well as the Federation meet. He finished third in the state meet and sixth in the eastern state championship. His best was a blistering 15:01 for the 3.1 mile course.

Casey went on to make a name for himself in the motion picture industry and earned a spot in the credits for several movies he worked on.

REGINA

Regina (Winky) was the cute one in face and form. She got her nickname because from the moment she came home from the hospital, she winked at everyone who looked at her. She was born with a caretaking attitude. After Mom passed away, she assumed the principle role of looking after Dad. He relied on her heavily and she always stood up to the task including calling him down when necessary. She developed some very close and loyal friends who she still has today.

Winky was always organized and eager to keep everything neat and in its place. She also was very matter of fact in her evaluation of various situations. One day she came home and showed Mom the grade she received for a project she worked hard on. Mom said, "That's great honey! You've got to be happy about the grade your teacher gave you!" Her reply: "She didn't give me nothin'! I worked my butt off for that and I deserve it!"

Winky had a good sense of humor and wasn't shy about telling stories about herself and her friends. I'll never forget how upset she got the time we all laid on the lawn at Jane's house and each swore we could see the American flag on the moon.

For several years Winky put her organizational skills to good use by being a travel agent. One of the perks of the job was the ability to travel and Winky enjoyed that to the fullest. Of all the kids, she has traveled the most hitting countries like Israel, Ireland, France, Mexico, several places on the continent of Africa, and all over the U.S.

-3-
TWO-LEGGED MISCHIEF, ADVENTURE, & MAYHEM

As kids we spent some time in front of the T.V. Our television featured black and white programs and was made of metal with a wood grain look. The knob on the side was large and thumped as you turned it. Our roof held an antenna with the Empire State building serving as a receiver. There was no need of cable back then as the "rabbit ears" on the top of the TV held aluminum foil to help with the reception. After 11 p.m. all programs were off, and the screen was occupied by a target-like picture with the channel prominently displayed in the center. In the morning, this was all that greeted viewers until the stations came back on.

When there was nothing else to do or we were in for the night we lounged in front of the entertainment box. The menu included, *Leave it to Beaver, Mr. Ed, Bonanza, Soupy Sales, The Smothers Brothers, Bewitched, Andy Griffith, I Love Lucy*, and the Sunday night Disney movies. When fear or intrigue were called for, *The Twilight Zone, Alfred Hitchcock*, and *Dark Shadows* were summoned.

Though we had our fill of television, we largely lived an outdoor life of games and adventure. Those were the days of holding someone down and repeatedly slapping their abdomen to ensure a "pink belly" or twisting the skin on their forearm to turn it red and label it an "Indian arm burn." Thumb wrestling and holding someone in a head lock while rubbing their scalp with one's knuckles (a noogie) were readily anticipated as part of the day's activities.

Birthday wishes were completed with "A kick to get sick and a pinch to grow an inch" Yes, those were well-wishes! Birthday parties were well attended, and we never expected the host family to give us a gift! We were just happy with some ice cream and cake and looked forward to games and singing that the "Hokey Pokey" was what it was all about!

The neighborhood was filled with kids of all ages. Families with two or three children were considered small families. Those with six kids were seen as normal. But two families within our town had particularly large families. The Dirtengers had eleven children and the Delias had thirteen. Because there were so many children in the Delia home, the parents thought it necessary to have a pay phone installed. Just within one block of our home there were no less than thirty-eight kids. This made large games easy to come by and most games ended with friends supplying a hard rap on the arm followed by the well-worn phrase, "Gotcha last!"

We played the usual neighborhood games like kick the can, freeze tag, flashlight tag, hide 'n seek, and the more organized games of football, basketball, softball, whiffle ball, and stick ball were all part of our schedule. The front yard of St. Aedan's Catholic church served as our unofficial playing field, and we never saw it as trespassing. Somehow, we thought it was acceptable to paint a strike zone on the side of the church building for hours of stick ball. I've since learned this is not trespassing—it's vandalism!

We played a game called "Out." With two to four players involved, we each took turns throwing a tennis ball as hard as we could against the wall. The next player was to catch the ball on one bounce. Failure to do so gave you one of the letters in the word "Out." When a player lost, his punishment was to stand against the wall with his hands protecting "the family jewels" while the other players each took a shot at throwing the ball at him. If he flinched, the throw didn't count.

When the call was for more aggressive games we played "King of the Mountain." The rules were very simple. You found a large pile of dirt and a person to start off as "The King." His job was to stand on top fending off the others trying to knock him off. If he was knocked off, the guy who dislodged him took his place.

"Kill the guy with the ball" was another simple but aggressive game. Boundaries were set up and whoever had the ball was knocked down until he gave it up to someone else. Then that person was tackled as well. In some ways it was a lot like rugby except there were no teams. It really was every man for himself! The game went on until someone got hurt or we all got too tired to continue.

"British Bulldog" was a little more organized but just as brutal. There were two lines on either end of the field. One person was in the middle and everyone else was behind one of the lines in the "safe zone." When the person in the middle said "British Bulldog, 1-2-3" everyone had to run from one line to the other without being tackled. The one who was tackled, became part of the Bulldogs. Thus, the numbers inside grew and the numbers outside shrank. If you were the last one left, you still had to make one more run across the mass of kids. And that was when things could get really rough. Often it ended with a "Dog pile." May God have mercy on the guy on the bottom!

Moments of boredom were rare but dangerous. It is said, "Idle hands are the devil's playground" and we spent lots of time in his playground. Sitting with Casey, Matt, and Billy might bring up a conversation something like this:

> *"What do you wanna do?"*
> *"I don't know. What do you wanna do?*
> *"I asked you first!"*
> *"I asked you second!"*
> *"Let's throw rocks at cars"*
> *"Okay!"*

We didn't always throw rocks. Sometimes it was snowballs or crabapples or dirt bombs. The point behind these foolish decisions was not necessarily to be destructive. The goal was to experience the challenge and excitement of being chased and getting away. It was the rush of adrenalin that we were after. The ultimate goal was to escape the chase of a teenager. In the nearby woods we claimed as our own, we had created several paths. This was our safe place! If we could reach the woods, we had an excellent chance of escape.

If my parents ever got wind of what we were doing, this would result in a near death beating followed by grounding. No matter how long I was grounded for, it was always too long. Incarceration for me was tantamount to cruel and unusual punishment.

There were different levels of discipline (also known as behavioral adjustment) in our home. The lowest form involved the look. It was a form Mom often used. She would furrow her brow and narrow her eyes and glare at you. If your Mom had "The Look" you know exactly what I mean. This look simply meant, "I see you and you're about to get into big trouble." Often, this is all it took to adjust our behavior.

The next level of discipline was the voice. Both Mom and Dad exercised these weapons. Being yelled at didn't hurt physically but the mental image that followed got your attention. A loud voice with the threat of violence most times did the trick. When very angry, Dad's favorite threat was, "I'll throttle you!" As a six- or seven-year-old, I had no idea what "throttle" meant, but I was certain it would be painful. Mom's verbal threat was a bit calmer but no less certain. She would put her hands on her hips, look us in the eye, and say, "I could cheerfully shoot you!" In my young mind, that simply meant that Mom was going to kill me and enjoy it too.

Often, the punishment was related to the crime. If you stole something from a store, you had to return it with an apology. If you hit someone, the board of education was applied to the seat of understanding. If your language was unacceptable, it was cleaned up with soap.

I tried to fight the soap deal by clamping my jaw shut and pursing my lips. Mom just couldn't loosen me up. She retreated to the kitchen and returned with a new invention perched on our sink— liquid soap! My punishment was delivered simply with a squirt of that stuff. Sometimes technological advances can work against you!

Most times Dad didn't wait to give us a swat. But when he did wait, it was just long enough to retrieve a belt from the closet. Mom's weapon of choice was a nearby wooden spoon, fly swatter, or a belt.

The worst type of punishment was in the category of a "Woopin.'" A "Woopin'" happens only in extreme cases. This is where Mom or Dad would catch a child by the arm with one hand and beat their bottom in a circle with a lecture that matched each pop with the syllable of their words. It might go something like this: "I" swat, "Told" swat, "You" swat, "Not" swat, "To" swat, "Flush" swat, "Your" swat, "Shirt" swat, "Down" swat, "The" swat "Toilet" swat!

In the end, the parent would be out of breath, worn out, and often still angry. The child would be turned loose in a pool of tears, a painful rump, and a bruised upper arm.

Back in the day, phones were attached to the lower wall by a long cord. To dial a number within the confines of Pearl River, you only needed to dial four numbers—4266 in our case. If you wanted to dial outside the area you had to use the assigned three digits. So, our number of "Pearl River 5, 4266" was 735-4266. Later, as the population swelled, you had to use an area code outside of your area. Today all ten numbers are needed to dial anywhere. Give me back my simple life!

One day, Mom was in the kitchen on the phone. She had a habit of opening the drawer, pulling the long cord into the kitchen, and using the drawer as a cradle to hold it. Then, she was somewhat free to do the work she was engaged in as she cradled the receiver between her shoulder and cheek.

Dorothy had locked me out of the house and was tormenting me with her teasing faces. I kept banging on the storm door, but my mother was too engrossed in her conversation to notice. Running to the front door changed nothing as Dot easily beat me there and locked that as well.

Finally, my temper got the best of me and in a rage, I crashed through the entire window of the storm door. That got Mom's attention! Of course, with Dorothy on the inside, the initial wrath of Mom was spent on her. In short order she turned her anger toward me. But I was off the steps and behind the neighbor's house before my enraged mother could give chase.

All roads lead back home, so I timidly made my way to the house. The glass was all cleaned up and Mom was seated on a chair in the living room. She still had the belt on her lap and when she saw me, I could see the anger returning to her face. This was sure to be one that blasted past one of those, "I could cheerfully shoot you" moments.

But then her face grew soft, and her natural color returned. I didn't understand it until I looked down and saw blood on my arms and shirt. I suppose the adrenalin rush brought on by the fear of death was so quick that I didn't notice that I had been injured. She took me to the bathroom sink and cleaned me up. The cuts weren't so bad and certainly preferable to the beating I thought I was destined for.

Not far from our home in different directions we discovered three haunted houses. The only requirements for a house to be labeled haunted were that it had to be deserted and run down. Exploring these houses gave us stories galore.

One house was on the corner of Middletown Road and Washington Avenue. It was a two-story house complete with broken windows and a couple of stray black cats (a sure sign). While on our way home after some time at the movies, Matt, Billy, Casey and I made our way toward the haunted house. Being confronted with the option of being in evil places brings to the forefront of your mind all the horror stories and movies you've ever heard or viewed. *House on Haunted Hill, Carrie, The Exorcist*, and others rise to the top as you are faced with the opportunity of thrills, chills, and spills.

With the usual dares and double dares, we all agreed to approach the house. We got in through the front door and worked our way around the main floor. There was nothing to be seen but a few pieces of abandoned furniture and some holes in the walls. We decided that a trip upstairs was called for, so we slowly worked our way up the wooden steps. They creaked with every step, giving further proof that ghosts really did live there. We moved slowly and quietly understanding that our lives were in danger and that death could follow at any moment. At the top of the steps, coming from one of the rooms, we heard something fall. That's all we needed. The race for the front door was on! I grabbed the doorknob only to find it come off in my hand. By the time I turned, Casey was part way out the window with Matt and Billy close behind. I'm sure we ran a quarter mile before we stopped to catch our breath and to give that nervous laugh which often follows close calls.

Another haunted house was found on Middletown Road as well. But this one was at the top of Manor Boulevard. This one wasn't nearly as scary except if the cops came, which they did more than once. Three of us gained entry through a side door in the basement carefully working our way up the stairs which had collapsed. The first time we entered this place we had to climb over books and piles of clothes. We got to the stairs and were just about to begin our ascent when a cat—of course a black one, jumped up on the keyboard of the piano. That had all our attention. We saw what happened immediately, so we didn't run. When we calmed down, we continued our climb up the stairs. An uneventful tour of the main floor was followed by a quick trip to the top floor.

We checked out each room but found nothing worth talking about. I was just about to head back down the stairs when my friend Stephen came racing down the hall pushing a desk. He pushed the desk past me and slammed it into the far wall. I still don't know why he did it. The corner of the desk hit the window breaking what was left of it. Then we saw the cop car outside. We were momentarily trapped! We kept our cool and waited until we knew he was in the house. When we saw his shadow in the stairwell, we made our move out the window and onto a lower roof. We made the short jump from the roof and were headed through an adjoining yard long before we heard the cop yell, "And don't come back!"

Down Townline Road, just beyond the entrance to the Palisades Parkway was the third of our haunted house venues. The two-story house was painted grey which had faded due to the elements of sun and time. Windows were cracked and boarded up, shades were torn, and the front porch was riddled with rotten boards. All this was definitive proof that this place was haunted. Billy, Casey, Matt, and I were making our way to the *40-Foot Hole* when we passed the place. We each promised to enter on our way back if the others would go with us.

During our return trip, as we drew nearer to the house, we began talking ourselves into going in. In nervous unison, we climbed the steps which creaked with every move eliminating any question about the house being occupied by spirits.

We stood together in front of the door understanding that our next move may lead to a direct encounter with a disgruntled ghost or deadly monster. No black cats this time. On the count of three, we turned the knob and bounced into the living room. I'm not sure who was more surprised, the four of us, or the six people sitting at the dining room table. All eyes turned in our direction and a millisecond later we were out on the sidewalk and racing for the safety of our homes.

A few blocks up Ehrhardt Road stood St. Stephen's Church. I remember spending time watching them building it. It was constructed so that from the top you could see the shape of a cross. There was a row of cherry trees near the road, and as you can imagine, we spent a good bit of time harvesting cherries from the branches. There was no question that this was a premeditated exercise as we showed up with buckets to engage in the activity. This of course was not allowed so when Mr. Fisher, who was connected to the church, came out, we scattered. We didn't go far however, because we had to come back and make a statement.

When the proverbial smoke cleared, we made our way back to the church and by a highly sophisticated method determined who would instigate "pay back." Often this method went something like this: We put our fists in a circle and each fist was tapped as the caller went around the circle calling out, "My mother and your mother were hanging out the clothes. My mother punched your mother right in the nose. What color blood came out?" The last person touched would call out any color they chose. Whatever color they chose was used to complete the selection. (I.e.: Green. "G-R-E-E-N spells green and you are it.") The person chosen would then have the task of running up to the entrance of the church and ringing the gigantic bell sitting on the raised porch. The mandate was that they had to swing the bell ringing it at least five times before running away. Often, we would stop by and ring the bell when retaliation wasn't called for. It just seemed like the thing to do while on our way to wherever we were headed.

One day, Casey was "the chosen one." Never to be outdone and wanting to show that he was worthy of hanging out with us, Casey began swinging the huge bell back and forth. He must have rung it fifteen times. He just wouldn't stop and run away. It wasn't until Mr. Fisher made his way across the lawn that he stopped and escaped cleanly. That day, Casey moved up a couple of notches in our acceptance book.

The church leaders eventually tired of the bell ringing going on. Perhaps the neighbors complained. But for whatever reason, the gong was removed from the bell. We were indignant. They never consulted us!

But this move never cut short our shenanigans. It only meant that it called for more sophisticated planning. On more than one occasion, one of us was chosen to ring the iconic bell. The method we used, a hammer. We had "borrowed" a hammer from Billy and Matt's garage and kept it hidden in the bushes not far from the church. When we were scheduled to pass by the church, a quick stop made us armed but not dangerous. Let the bells ring out!

Bear Mountain was a particularly attractive place. It is located north of Pearl River by about twenty miles. The short trip up the Palisades Parkway opens one up to a huge inn, athletic fields, a skating rink, water sports, a zoo, pool, and a walking trail around Hessian Lake. The Hessians were German mercenaries who were hired by the British to fight for them during the Revolutionary War. On October 6, 1777, 250 Hessian soldiers joined a large group of English soldiers and worked their way to Bear Mountain to launch an attack on Fort Montgomery and Fort Clinton which were seated on the north side of Bear Mountain. The colonists held them off and threw the dead bodies of the Hessians into the lake. Afterwards the name of the lake was called "Bloody Lake" or "Hessian Lake."

The area carries with it other fascinating stories of the Revolutionary War, along with the fictional story of Rip Van Winkle. From different parts of the property one can see the iconic Bear Mountain Bridge crossing over the majestic Hudson River. The opposite side of the bridge leads you to the place where Major John Andre (British) and General Benedict Arnold (Colonialist) were captured as Andre carried the plans to West Point in his boot. Benedict Arnold escaped but Major Andre was tried, convicted of spying, and hanged in Tappan, just south of Pearl River. Way, way back in the day, justice was swift and certain.

Our backyard held two willow trees. Over time we lost one but the other one provided lots of opportunity for recreation. Besides simply climbing, we mounted a pulley at the top. We ran a rope through the pulley and tied a board at the other end. A large knot was tied in the middle of the rope to snag in the pulley with the rest of the rope running to the ground. With the branches of a willow being so flexible, we could hoist someone up to the top of the tree and let him go. He would come flying down and enjoy a cushion-like stop at the bottom. Of course, we decided that it had to be part of an initiation to be able to hang out with us. From the road in the front of the house, a person could look over the garage and see a participant sitting on a board at the top of the tree. Moments later he would witness that same person flying down and disappear when the other end was loosed. Our neighbor, Jane, called it "instant heart attack."

One day my brother Casey became the brunt of our humor. We talked him into mounting the board then brought him to the top. Minutes later we had tied the other end to the base of the tree and were off to find something else to do. When we checked on him a good while later, he was still in place and seemed to be enjoying both the shade and the view.

Back in the day, Little League was a big deal and it seemed that when the season started, all roads led to Anderson Fields. The league started in 1953 and still operates today. The fields are found in the original location on Hunt Road in Orangeburg. There were three divisions, T-ball, international league, and the majors. I played for four years and was on the Americans, Minutemen, and the Wildcats (two years). Every eye was on the majors and every boy had it in his heart that one day he would play there.

Those hot summer days were filled with friendships and fun as we battled it out each Saturday. The Major League fields housed the snack bar and featured everything from hot dogs and soda to Italian ice. Every Saturday without exception and several times during the day, the loudspeakers would blare "Winchester Cathedral." Yes, I still remember the tune and a lot of the words—this could be listed as brain washing. At the international fields, a motivated kid could climb the fence behind home plate and get his fill of foul balls. We were never at a loss for baseballs in our neighborhood.

It doesn't matter where you go, or how old you are, one thing is for certain, parents can often take the GAME way too seriously. It's more than obvious that each kid has a really good shot at playing pro ball one day—yeah right!—Are you kidding me? So, it's understandable how a parent can become a "hyper-fan." One day, I came up to bat and heard my mother and a man in the stands behind home plate, getting into it. She was holding my buddy Franky's little sister Alice, and this man was yelling at her. The crowd calmed things down, but for a fleeting moment, I actually wondered if I should defend my mother with the bat in my hand.

I also witnessed things getting out of hand when during tryouts (6th grade) the father of one of my classmates showed up with his son and ordered his son to beat up another boy. The two boys had gotten into it in school and this man's son was bested by the other boy. I stared in amazement as the man tried to hold back all the other dads so his son could beat this other kid up. Just another episode in the category of ARE YOU KIDDING ME?

The skill level of each of the players ranged from those the team could count on to those who couldn't catch a dish rag. Eric was one of the better skilled players. He played third base in T-ball. One day, I watched in admiration as he scooped up a shot hit down the line, and with the ball still in his glove, ran down the runner heading for home tagging him out. It was a major league play, and no one wondered why he only spent one year in the international league before being called up to the majors.

Sportsmanship was always encouraged. After each game, both teams would gather by their respective dug outs and holler, "Two, four, six, eight, who do we appreciate? the ___, the ___, hooray!" But kids being what they are, the winning team often substituted one word completely changing the meaning: "Two, four, six, eight, who did we assassinate, the___, the ___, hooray!"

Because baseball was so big in our lives, so was collecting baseball cards. Five cards came in a pack along with a flat piece of pink bubble gum. Several packs were opened at the same time with the cards being stacked into a single pile. The gum went into your mouth first before thumbing through your cards in search of a treasure. While chewing the gum, a common phrase was used, "Got it. Got it. Want it. Need it. Got it. Need it..." Trading immediately followed.

I had a shoe box full of cards. We didn't understand the value of the cards and thoughts of selling them never crossed our minds. I wish I had my box of cards today. I had Lou Gehrig, Hank Aaron, and "The Mick." And yes, I had more than one Babe Ruth.

One of our favorite activities with our cards was in fact, gambling. We had three games we played. "Farsies" which meant you competed against another boy to see how far you could throw your card. To throw a card, you held it between the index and middle fingers. When your arm came forward a snap of the wrist sent the small piece of pictured cardboard sailing like a Frisbee. The one who outdistanced the other got to keep his opponent's card. Of course, the penalty of possession was retrieval.

We also played a game called, "Nearsies." Each player stood a designated distance from a wall or step. You took turns tossing your card as close as possible to the wall or step. The closest one wins the other player's card. A "Leaner" was an automatic win unless the other player also tosses a "Leaner." At that point it was a tie. Both games could be played by a number of players.

But "Odds and Evens" could only be played by two players at a time. While standing next to each other, you each chose odds or evens and flipped your cards. Both landing face up or down was even and one face up and the other face down was odd. We found out early on, that if we played any of these games during school time, our cards would be confiscated by the fun-destroying teachers.

They must have known about it, but I still can't imagine why my parents would be okay with their thirteen-year-old son going with my classmate Jimmy to a baseball game in the Bronx. I had only been to NYC a few times in my life and each of those were with my parents. But there we were, sitting on the bus heading for Yankee Stadium. The Yankees were playing the Minnesota Twins and we were seated along the first base line on a hot and humid July afternoon. We gorged ourselves on hot dogs, cokes, and peanuts. We were young teens in heaven.

I spent a good bit of time looking alternately from home plate to a spot on the upper deck of the stadium. There were columns that came in an arch-like fashion around the outfield and over the crowd. On one of those arches was a mark commemorating the place that Mickey Mantle hit with one of his 536 home runs. It was done on May 11, 1963, and was over 565 feet. Historians claim that the ball was still on the rise when it struck the façade. I sat there in stunned amazement wondering how it was possible to hit a ball that far. His bat must have been laced with gun powder.

When the game was over, we came to the frightening realization that we didn't have enough money to take the bus home. We were fairly certain that we had enough to get us from the George Washington Bridge to home, but we were equally certain that we didn't have enough coin to take the same route that got us there.

We grabbed a handful of relish packs from the snack bar and

began our two and a half mile trek to the bridge. I had no idea where we were going and put my full trust in Jimmy to navigate our way. I knew the entire time that I was out of place and kept my head on a swivel as we quickly worked our way across the Harlem River, through Upper Manhattan, Harlem, and Washington Heights. I was never so happy to see the GW bridge in my life. We found the right bus and slept most of the way home. We arrived safely in Pearl River, feeling richer for the adventure and a win by the Yanks.

He came in completely invited and created. He was "Charlie" I have no idea how he got his name, but he was a literal dummy. By sewing pants to a shirt and coloring a Clorox bottle for a head, and stuffing him with old newspapers, Charlie came to life.

Charlie was the source of endless entertainment. Sometimes you would find him in a backyard tree. At other times he was on the front steps. Often, he would be found sitting on a bike in the front yard. When not the center of entertainment, he would lie dormant until moments of boredom brought him to activity and adventure.

John and Jeff found some amusement by laying Charlie in the road with ketchup on his chest, while the two boys lay next to him. One at a time as a car came down Manor Boulevard, the boys would get up and run. All the cars stopped in front of Charlie waiting for him to move. They then yelled at my brothers and drove around him.

One time though, some fun-loving teens sped up scaring Charlie into running as well. But Charlie never moved. Way too late the brakes were applied, and they skidded over our over-stuffed friend. Jumping from the car in a panic, they knelt to find Charlie under the car. Their cursing could be heard from four blocks away.

Another time, Charlie was the center of entertainment when several of us were in a circle on the edge of Ehrhardt road. The cars were coming by at a good speed and by a foolish plan we began to push each other back and forth as a car would approach. At a pre-planned point someone would throw Charlie into the road and "Wham!" the car would hit Charlie and the driver would skid to a panicked stop. As fast as the driver would look back, the lawn was empty of our young and foolish lives.

Mrs. Merle was an old German lady who was hired by my parents (one time) to look after us while they went out to a social event. I'm not good at guessing ages now so I'm sure I was bad at it then. In my young mind, she seemed to be about 200 years old. Certainly, she was too old to look after six Jirgalettes. To no one's surprise, Jeff (ten years old), was acting up. Mrs. Merle sent him to his room. My father had built a laundry chute going from the upstairs to the basement ending in front of the washer with an opening on the main floor. In anger and seeking revenge, Jeff yelled down the chute, "Mrs. Merle, Mrs. Merle! I'm going to jump down the laundry chute and kill myself and it's gonna be your fault!" When poor Mrs. Merle opened the chute door, down came Charlie in a flash. This elderly undeserving German lady screamed in terror and panic—though she never went downstairs to check on Jeff's *dead body*. Soon my parents came home to find a crying Mrs. Merle at the kitchen table. "Dey vas very Bohd!" "What happened" my Dad asked. "Jeffy jumped down the laundry chute! Jeffy is dead!" My father turned to see Jeff coming down the stairs. In a stern voice my father asked, "Jeffrey, did you jump down the laundry chute?" "No!" Jeff replied. "Don't lie to me. Did you go down the laundry chute?" my Dad pressed. Shrugging his shoulders Jeff said, "It wasn't me. It was Charlie!" In seconds my father put it all together and did his best not to smile. All he could get out was, "We'll deal with this later." And they did though it was by normal standards very mild.

One day as a first grader, I came home from school to find that Mom had missed a couple of days of addressing the laundry. With eight people living in one home, the laundry could become overwhelming quickly. Looking down the chute, I found the laundry piled up almost to the mouth of the chute. In excitement I told my brother Jeff. I suggested that we could go now down the chute without getting hurt.

Moments later I found myself on the end of a rope moving down the chute. I must have made a good bit of noise because it brought my mother to the opening on the main floor. When she opened the chute door, she found a taught rope in the opening. "What's is going on?" she yelled. With those words, the rope lost its tension and I found myself crashing through the hamper and slamming into the washing machine. Jeff got a spanking and I got sympathy for a bruised head. My Mom later asked me, "Weren't you scared?" My reply: "Not 'til you showed up."

Charlie came back into use in another special episode. There was a special designated day in the town of Pearl River. It was called "Junk Day." This was a day where anyone could put anything out by the curb and the town would come by and collect it. It took a long time for the trucks to make the rounds so things stayed by the road for several days. For us kids, this was a time of treasure hunting. Jumping on our bikes we would scan the surrounding area for items that were worth keeping. We found lawn mower engines that were re-purposed for Go-Karts. We discovered lamps that could be re-wired and sold for a few bucks. One time I found a mink stole that my mother bought from me, had it dry cleaned and gave it to her mother.

Lil was an Irish lady—complete with a strong Irish brogue. She lived across the street and she and my mother were good friends. The two of them would spend hours at the kitchen table or in the den trading stories and ideas. Mom explained to her that junk day was coming the next day, and how the system worked.

The following day Lil had placed a red chair, a stand-up lamp, and a few small items by the edge of her driveway. Mom got a call later that day from Lil informing her that someone had taken the chair. Our neighbor Kenny had a toilet that had cracked, and not having anything by his curb, he decided to put in with Lil's pile. The next call from Lil informed my mother about the toilet. "They've taken me chair and dropped off a terlet! It's not junk day, it's put-n- take day!"

Seizing the opportunity for a good laugh, I put Charlie to work. In short order I had Charlie on Lil's toilet with an open newspaper in his hands. A call again to my mother from Lil followed. "Reggie, I came down the driveway and found a man on me terlet! There's a man outside on me terlet!" Mom looked out the front window and spotted Charlie in all his glory. "Isn't that hilarious? she said. Lil's respond was classic, "I wet me pants!"

While in college I received a package from home (how I cherished any mail I got). When I opened it, I found an unstuffed Charlie with a note from my Mom, "Have fun with Charlie! He's not the first dummy who ever went to college!" But that's another Charlie story for another book.

Most of the elementary schools were neighborhood schools,

so the early morning saw hundreds of children meandering their way to school. Nauraushaun, Lincoln Avenue, Central Avenue, and Evans Park were the town's elementary schools. I attended Evans Park with Ms. Ruth Jersey giving me my first introduction to formal education. She seemed to be very old but was loving and kind.

I was so centrally focused I didn't know there were other schools in town. Most of us carried bag lunches with a nickel to buy a carton of milk which came with a paper straw that was sure to collapse before the milk was consumed. By second grade my friend Glenn had introduced me to the idea of bringing in a sandwich bag of powdered chocolate. For the rest of my elementary days, I enjoyed chocolate milk with my lunch.

The first day of first grade was an eye-opening experience. Our teacher, Mrs. Renc asked if anybody needed to go to the lavatory. None of us had ever heard that word before so what we heard was "laboratory." That got our attention and several of us raised our hands. It seemed like a cruel joke. We were expecting test tubes, electric wires, and a Bunsen burner. We got a sink, a stall, and a wall full of urinals.

It was in first grade at Evans Park Elementary school that I learned that our P.E. teacher, Mr. Schletter, and I didn't have the same sense of humor. We were all gathered in the gym which also served as the cafeteria, taking turns climbing up the rope to the ceiling. The line went out into the hall and passed the row of light switches for the gym. As a boy was at top of the rope and about to ring the mounted bell in victory, the temptation was too much for me to bear. So, I put my forearm on the entire set of switches and with the speed of electricity the gym was darkened.

With equal speed the lights were turned back on, and I was in the grasp of an angry Mr. Schletter. I can still feel the pain on the side of my face as he grasped my fledgling sideburns between his thumb and forefinger. I'm not sure what he said, but the pain on the side of my face brought my mind to agreement with him. I never did that again.

Halloween was an abnormally great day for us. It meant racing from door to door to beg for sweet treats. Often, we would be knocking on the doors of the very same homes we vandalized the night before.

Traditionally, the night before Halloween was called "Gate Night." It was so called because in its origination, the pranksters would switch the gates of the sidewalks of different homes. Homeowners would wake up to find a red gate where a white gate was the previous day. Gates in front of homes were no longer the norm, so *Gate Night* transitioned into *Mischief Night*. Soaping car windows, smashing pumpkins, and popping doors with flour-filled socks were in vogue.

One Gate Night Franky and I decided it would be a good prank to lay over the Barnhart's decorative well house. It wasn't attached to anything so with a team effort we were able to dislodge it from its base. Quietly and gently, we tilted the square well. Our plan was to leave it on its side and run away. But as the well tilted more and more it got heavier and heavier and simply got away from us. Down it went and as it hit the ground the entire roof came off. Running like the wind came without suggestion. This writing is the first official confession of that prank.

It's not wise to leave your car unlocked overnight, and on one occasion a neighbor found that to be true. In stealth manner, Pat and I taped Mr. Lengio's car horn down. The car horn blared for at least five minutes and once again we got away without punishment.

But when Halloween day arrived all mischief was sidelined That was a day of dressing up and getting out to fill your stores with candy. My parents were very creative in getting us ready for the day. Our costumes took time and creativity. One year I was painted green and went out as the "Green Giant" complete with green fabric cut up to resemble leaves. John turned heads when he came out as Dracula and Jeff was a cannibal wearing a wooden mask my Dad made for him.

Some kids carried decorative paper bags, but not us! Paper tore too easily and didn't hold up well for the running we did and the long stretch of time we were out. So, we carried pillowcases. Our goal was to work our way up to the Marigold Apartments about a half mile away. We knew that at the apartments we could hit each of the four doors on each floor and turn to the first that opened. Then we'd race to the next floor and the next before making it to the adjoining building. In minutes we had hit up dozens of homes for our sweet reward.

When we got home, Mom would have to inspect our haul. Anything not wrapped was quickly thrown out. Though undocumented, there were too many stories of crazy people poisoning children or putting razor blades in apples. Mom also charged us a tax for letting us go out. The fee was candy corn. It was her favorite, so she obligated us to give a share of our candy corn. There were some years when my stash of candy would last beyond the beginning of the new year.

For several years I never went to school the day after Halloween. Invariably, my mother would see me eating a lot of candy and tell me to stop because it would make me sick. I only had to hear that one time to get the grey matter in my head working.

Before I went to sleep, I would set my alarm clock for an early morning rise. I'd make my way down to my mother's bedside and let her know I had a stomach-ache. She'd shake her head in a sleepy way and mildly scold me for eating too much candy. Then she'd send me back to bed and I'd have the day off. My stomach *still hurt* when I woke up, but invariably the sickness would wear off by the time it was too late to go to school. Miracles do happen!

Of course, I wasn't the only kid to fake being sick to find freedom from school. Some of my friends developed very creative ways to garner a holiday. While leaving school one day, my friend Frank informed me that there would be no school for him the next day. I asked him what he was going to do, and he let me know his plans. We stopped by Food Fair, and he bought a can of cream of chicken soup for a dime. After dinner that night, he would go into the bathroom and make "throw-up" sounds. When his mother came in, she found the toilet filled with "vomit" and he would be sent to bed with the promise of no school the next day.

Christmas day was a day filled with magic. At our home we had decorations outside but very little on the inside. Besides hanging our stockings, which were all hand-made, we put nothing up—no tree, no lights, no ornaments, no presents—nothing. We went to bed on Christmas Eve with "Hopes that St. Nicholas soon would be there." Coming down early—and sometimes very early, we found a tree full of ornaments and lights. And the presents! With eight in our family, there was a mountain of presents and our stockings were so full the threads were screaming for mercy. In the kitchen we found a table dressed in lace and ready for us to enjoy a special meal. The only thing we could open before breakfast was our stockings. Breakfast always included coffee, tea, English muffins, jelly, scrambled eggs, and link sausage.

One Christmas morning I awoke to discover the unbelievable. I was the recipient of a brand new shiny black Schwinn bicycle. Never in my life had I owned a new bike. I was always the possessor of hand-me-downs and used toys. This present far exceeded my expectations and I couldn't wait until all the gift opening was over so I could take my new ride for a test drive. Later that morning, after a few falls, it finally sunk in that bike tires don't travel well over ice. I was forced to do the unthinkable—wait.

In later years my father informed me that there were several Christmas days when they went to bed twenty minutes before we got up. When breakfast was finished, someone was assigned the duty of bringing a trash can for all the wrappings. Then the youngest child who could read would retrieve a present and deliver it to each of us one at a time. Only one present was opened so we all had a chance to enjoy each other's gifts. Several times I would look over at Mom and Dad and see that their faces were lit up with the satisfaction of once again bringing happiness our way. The rest of the day was spent enjoying the gifts we received.

Because a large percentage of the town's population was Italian and Irish, St. Patrick's Day was another huge day in Pearl River. Family names like Mahoney, O'Reilly, Murphy, O'Sullivan, Kelly, McPartland, and O'Conner were in abundance. New York City hosted the largest St. Patrick's Day parade in the country. I think Pearl River hosted the second largest. The traditional parade had been in place for almost thirty years and attracted over 20,000 people. The entire town seemed like it was buzzing. A green line was painted in the middle of the parade route that went down Middletown Road and Central Avenue. It seemed like everyone, and anyone, was in the parade and the long line of participants felt like it lasted for hours.

The fire department, police department, high school bands, politicians, unions, businesses, ambulance corp, and others proudly marched in front of flag waving and cheering families that lined the streets the entire length of the route. Friends and families tailgated and barbequed in the parking lots along the way. Of course, alcohol flowed like a river, but no one seemed to get out of hand. It was just a good old celebration of heritage and a great time of socializing with friends and family.

Being half Irish (Mom was a pure bred with Monaghan for a maiden name), St. Patrick's Day was big in our family as well. We grew up with so many Irish tales and songs. Songs like, "When Irish Eyes are smilin'", "Dirty Lil," "Danny Boy" and "I'm a rambler, I'm a gambler" were often heard coming from my Mom and before it became *uncool* the rest of us kids joined in. My nickname was McGee (an Irish tinker), and my sister Dorothy was called Pooka.

The name Pooka comes from an Irish tale of a large invisible rabbit who would visit homes after a party. During the night the Pooka would clean up while the family was asleep. In payment for the work, the Pooka would eat and drink all the leftovers. One night a family forgot about the Pooka showing up and they cleaned up the house before retiring. Upon finding the house in order and nothing to eat or drink the Pooka became enraged and trashed the place. This was no reflection on my sister Dorothy.

My father had made my mother a tall flagpole for the front yard. Most days it displayed the American flag. But on St. Patrick's Day the Irish flag was proudly hoisted. When we awoke on this special day, we found that one of the "Wee People" had visited our home and turned all our milk green. It was a great surprise and cemented an unforgettable memory into our hearts and minds.

The Fourth of July was another big day in the town of Pearl River. Usually, another parade was scheduled and another opportunity to celebrate was engaged. Fireworks exploded in abundance with the usual unannounced competition of who had the greatest explosions. Back then you could buy mats or blocks of firecrackers, bottle rockets, cherry bombs, M80's (which were an 8th stick of dynamite), and a plethora of rockets. Going to town or driving over to the field at Nanuet High School was a big treat and the display seemed to last forever always ending with "The big finale."

We also celebrated on our own. Lots of parties could be found with friends and family getting together. We would tie several firecrackers together to heighten the noise. Blowing up things with a cherry bomb or M80 was always a thrill.

My brother John's friend David had blown off three of his fingers and as a young boy I tried not to stare but was always fascinated by his deformed hand. Early on the morning of the fifth, my brother Jeff and I would sneak into the back yards of several neighbors who had parties and scarf up the firecrackers that hadn't exploded. We gained a healthy stash this way.

Going to town with Mom or Dad was a special event. Mel's Army/Navy, Ben Franklin's "Five and Dime" the pet store, Hadler's Hardware, and other stores were favorite stops for my parents, and we were happy to tag along. Often, my mother would go into a store and turn us loose to play in the park in the center of town.

By the Post Office was a grassy area with benches, trees, and flower gardens. None of that appealed to us. When we thought about that park, one thing alone came to mind—the cannon. There was a huge silver cannon that always seemed to be freshly painted which was in the center of the park area. We climbed all over that piece of equipment, letting our minds run as wild as our young hearts would let them and stopping only long enough to watch the nearby commuter train move out. These days, I don't believe any parent would feel safe turning their kids loose like that. But eventually Mom would show up and find us on that cannon busying ourselves with killing some foreign enemy and saving the world.

We had two volunteer fire departments in our town—the Pearl River Hook and Ladder, and The Excelsior Fire Department. The annual firemen's carnival was a huge deal. It was a fund raiser the men held each year on the open field in the center of town. To my young mind, this was the greatest place on earth. Once we saw the posters stapled to telephone poles that's all we focused on. For weeks before the carnival arrived, our conversations defaulted to it.

We were saving our money to buy enough tickets to ride every ride. There were lots of rides, but we only concerned ourselves with the ones that carried an element of danger. The Ferris Wheel moved quickly and gave you that sense of falling. It moved both forward and backward. The "Whip" was a ride that carried you horizontally but moved each car in a circle as it threatened to crash you into the other cars. The challenge was to endure the force that pushed you against the sidewall of your car. On the "Round Up" or "Tilt Awhirl" each person stood up against a circular wall. The ride began to spin faster and faster and the outward force held you against the wall. Then the entire ride would tilt, and you would go 'round and 'round while also going up and down in the circle. It was without question, a "throw up" ride. A variation of this is the one where the riders spin in a circle and then the floor drops out while they are pinned against the wall. When nausea reaches the spinning rider's stomach, there is only one place for the vomit to go...all over the sick one and probably making its way to those nearby.

But none of the rides, absolutely none of the rides compared to "The Octopus." On this ride the victims are seated two to a car on the end of the arms of the Octopus. The ride spins you in a circle, brings you around the wider circle of the parameter, while simultaneously bringing you up and down. It is nothing short of terrifying and the faint of heart need not apply.

It took two summers before me, Casey, and any of our buddies worked up enough nerve to ride the Octopus. But when we did, the ride did not disappoint. Each of us saw our lives young pass before our eyes and we talked about it for weeks afterward.

Another summertime point of excitement was "Pearl River Days." This was a scheduled Saturday in which the main streets were closed to traffic and all the merchants in the downtown area moved their shops onto the sidewalks. There was food, music, and special sales. For us kids, it was a great time to go to town, meet up with other friends, and just hang out.

One day in sixth grade, Franky came over with some exciting news. He had come across the recipe for gun power. He explained that we could make gun power from sulfur, salt peter, and charcoal. Without debate, we got started gathering the ingredients. I raided my brother John's chemistry set and found the sulfur. We got the charcoal from our garage and within a half hour bought the salt peter from the pharmacy on central avenue. We mixed it up and in short order were in the woods behind Franky's house. His father had built a wooden bridge across the creek so he could dump his yard waste in the woods. (Can you see where this is heading?)

We made a six-inch wide pile of gun powder in the middle of the bridge with a long tail to give us time to seek cover and protect us from the coming explosion. (Safety always counts—yeah right!) We lit the tail and jumped behind a fallen log peaking up every few seconds to view the progress of the flame. The flame didn't move as we had hoped but it made its way to the pile. Of course, when it hit the pile, it didn't explode but gave a hollow and muffled "boom." A huge mushroom cloud followed quickly floating above the treeline. We had no choice but to run. We worked our way through the woods and within minutes were on the road a block away collaborating our story. Looking back, we could still see the cloud above the trees. A few minutes later we heard the sirens of the fire engines coming our way. If asked we had decided our story would be one of denial volunteering that "We saw some high school kids running away!" Our "experiment" resulted in a large hole being burned through the bridge. I got away without punishment, but Franky must have cracked. He was grounded for a week.

One summer day I found myself in possession of an M80. I wasn't sure what to do with it, but I knew I had to think it through. I wanted to do something big because I didn't want this gem to go to waste. Somehow, I decided to set it off in the empty basement storage area of St. Aedan's Catholic Church. In the past, I had dropped several firecrackers through the grate and enjoyed the increased boom caused by the echo, but I knew this one would be different. I placed it on the grate with the fuse holding it in place. When the fuse burned, it would drop to the floor and explode. Even though I stepped back from the grate, I wasn't quite ready for the noise. When it went off it sounded like a stick of dynamite. My head was buzzing, and I couldn't hear well. But those issues were secondary to the fact that I knew the police would be on their way. In a panic I headed for the safety and security of the woods, and I got away only being punished by a slight headache.

The holidays were also a reason for the neighborhood to party together. Often, we would host parties at our home. My parents got a keg of beer for the adults and a keg of birch beer for us kids. But the big party, the one that had us all talking for weeks prior and weeks after was the "Block Party." I was never certain if the name came from blocking off the street, or due to the fact that the entire block was invited, but I was certain that I would be there and that the fun would last the entire day. By petitioning the town, you could gain the right to block off the street at each end, and for the day, have a party in the street. For several years around the same time, we erected a barricade at the bottom of Manor Boulevard and at the intersection of Manor and Lang Terrace.

I don't know who organized it, but at the appointed time picnic tables, chairs, food, and grills appeared. It was a great time of playing games, listening to stories, and eating and drinking.

On one particular day, one of the older kids named Pat decided to help the charcoal grill move along in its duty. He took a can of gasoline—you can guess what happened—and poured it on the coals. The fire leaped from the grill and traveled up the stream of gasoline. Within seconds the can was aflame. In a panic, Pat threw the can of gas on a nearby lawn engulfing the front yard in flames. The men jumped into action and quickly extinguished the fire. The owners hadn't moved into the house so there were no further issues. Ironically the family moving in were named Burns and Pat's father was an active member of the fire department.

When I was about age twelve, my brother John invited me to join him during the trapping season. I really didn't want to do it, but I wanted to be with John and had a desire to impress him. I think he taught me more about nature and the outdoors than anyone else. It was decided that we would run a trap line in the large, wooded area off Blauvelt Road in the adjoining town of Nanuet. Our line covered about three miles. It was also decided that we would alternate turns in checking the line each evening. Somehow John was covered up with activities and it seemed like it was always my turn to do the deed. We caught muskrats, possum, squirrels, raccoons, and one undesirable and unforgettable skunk. We used a combination of foot traps and conibear traps (which killed instantly). As I was working the line, my nose told me that there was not good news up ahead. I could smell the skunk a good way off and remembered that it was a foot trap that we had placed in the area. Everything in me wanted to let him go, but there was no way to do that. I raced home, got a .22 rifle, and came back to claim the animal. We never wasted a fur and the task fell to me to skin it. I'm sure the smell of skunk lingered on my skin for two weeks!

When my brother Jeff announced to Casey and me that he had a cool idea we were all in before we learned the details. He led us to a place in the woods where John had deposited the skinless carcass of a possum. Just after dark, we put the possum in a bag and made our way up the street and around the corner. Moments later we had posed the possum upright on Brockman's doorstep. Mr.

Brockman was the Superintendent of the Pearl River school system which made the prank even greater. A quick knock on the door and a dash for the bushes followed. Mrs. Brockman came out, saw the hideous creature, and let out the scream we were looking for.

Cub Scouts was a great period in my life. All the boys in our family were members of the scouts. Our Dad was the pack master, so we were more than just a little involved. My Dad built the pinewood derby track and helped us with our cars. We came up with the design and then Dad, with a few modifications, walked us through building it. I built some cars for speed and some for show. One year I made a covered wagon that won a prize for originality.

Selling Cub Scout candy was a big deal with prizes for the most sales. I spent plenty of time going door to door so I could win. My mother would drop me off in a neighborhood and I would work through every house until I made my way home. It always paid off and twice I won first prize for the most sales.

We had a very active den. Cory, Pete, Frankie, Steve, Michael, and Bob are just a few of the names I recall. Although there was some kind of rule that prevented camping overnight until you were old enough to enter Boy Scouts, my Dad seemed to ignore it. He took our den on several overnight trips. On one trip, we traveled to North Lake. We went on a fairly long hike arriving back at camp in time to start a fire just before nightfall. After a great meal, we hunkered down in our tents for an uncomfortable night's sleep while the men sat around the fire and enjoyed sips of brandy and great conversation. The morning greeted us with twelve inches of snow, and we had to push the cars out to get home.

One of our trips was to the Ramapo Mountains. We found the trail that would lead us to Claudius Smith's den. Claudius Smith was a loyalist during the revolutionary war. He and his band of thieves (nicknamed "the cowboys") would come down from the mountains a raid the homes below. They stole cattle, horses, and anything of value they could get their hands on. One of the passageways opens up in the face of the mountain and the bandits could see from their perch any approaching people. Legend has it that Smith's mother told him that he would die with his boots on. This was to say, he would die a violent death. The story holds that before he was hung in 1779, he said, ""Mother often said I would die like a trooper's horse with my shoes on; but I will make her a liar." Then he kicked his boots off just before he was hanged. The rumor is that his loot is still buried in the surrounding area of the caves. You know what we spent some of our time doing.

It was at Claudius Smith's den that I learned two great things; I learned to put complete trust in my Dad, and I learned to repel. As we made our way up the trail, I wasn't sure why my Dad was carrying such a long rope, but I learned later that it was to teach us all how to repel down the side of the mountain. Without the proper gear, Dad just donned a pair of gloves and ran the rope across his shoulders. As I went over the edge, I remember his instructions to lean back and relax. These are words that are diametrically opposed. When you're fifty feet off the surface of solid rock, relaxing doesn't come easy.

About three miles from our home was an adventuring boy's dream. It was called the *40-Foot Hole*. I doubt that the water was forty feet deep so I'm guessing its name came from the height of the train trestle that ran above it. This was the place to fish, swim, and hunt for wildlife. Snakes, turtles, frogs, crayfish, and lizards could be found in abundance and provided hours of excitement for young boy's hearts.

Besides the *40-Foot Hole*, the train trestle was a place to hang out. Dad took us on several hikes down the abandoned tracks and across the trestle. He always had a pocket full of butterscotch candy which he shared with us as soon as we finished the last one. The tracks eventually lead to the *40-Foot Hole*. As you walked down the tracks from Blauvelt Road, the landscape began to drop down. This told us that we were getting closer and closer to our destination. As you walked across the bridge you could see through the ties and down to the water below. It was only about twenty feet but seemed like one hundred. Of course, we spent a good bit of time throwing things off the trestle and Dad told stories meant to scare us, but they mostly made us laugh.

Dropping down the hill from the trestle brought us to the stream that led to Henry Kaufmann's Campground. The campground was a large, wooded camp that encompassed almost one hundred acres. It featured a large lake, petting zoo, canoes, swimming pools, athletic fields, climbing areas, and volleyball courts. It was no wonder that as kids we were drawn to that place. The number of times we were escorted from the property goes beyond counting. More than once, we crossed the road from "Silver Rocks" (more on that later) and hid beneath the low branches of some trees to cast our lines in the pond. Huge carp with plenty of fighting power could be found there and the reward was worth the risk. Truth be told, sometimes we went there just to be chased from the place.

For our family to have a pool, we had to order sand. When the truck delivered a pile of sand it became the source of a great place to play. Billy and I were playing with our green army men all over the mound. We both had about the same number of guys, and we took turns defending the fort on top. We sunk firecrackers all over the sides of the mound to heighten the warfare. After the first couple of explosions, we gave up that idea as we both were covered with "shrapnel."

One day Billy came over with a brand new, bag of men—reinforcements from a store named L.H. Martins. My guys were outnumbered 3-1 and overpowered. I lost the first battle but came up with a plan that gave me a victory the next day. I went downstairs and got out the woodburning kit. I put a flat attachment on it and melted each of my guy's helmets automatically making them into Green Berets. The ratio changed immediately as we all know that one Green Beret equals ten regular soldiers.

Somehow, we came up with the idea that we should build a tunnel in the pile of sand. Billy and I took turns digging our way through the sand. Then when Billy was waste deep in the tunnel, the inevitable cave-in happened. Billy was kicking with everything he was worth, and I grabbed a shovel and began digging in a panic. I was too aggressive with my efforts and raised a good size horizontal lump on the back of my friend's head, but... he's alive today! Disaster was averted and a lesson was learned.

I know that lots of kids go to work with their fathers. Some go to an office, a retail store, or an outdoor work venue. Others go to a factory or a school. But I would contend that there is nothing, absolutely nothing better than showing up on a movie set or in a studio. There's so much to do and see. And when you're in the place where you witness how the movies or shows you've watched are made, it's unbeatable. Beyond that, sometimes you get to view a movie on T.V. that you watched in production.

A few times Dad took me to work with him. It didn't matter what he was doing, all I knew was that this seven-year-old boy was going to work with Dad and a big time was sure to follow. Two of those trips with Dad stand out in my mind.

One Saturday night Dad told me that in the morning he was going to shoot a commercial in a place called "Coney Island." He asked if I wanted to go and I said, "Yes" before he offered an explanation. We made the hour and a half trek, and I watched as my father mounted a camera on the front of a roller coaster named "The Cyclone." Within an hour they were ready for the shoot. Then my father asked me if I wanted to ride the coaster with him. I had never been on a roller coaster and didn't know what to expect. I was very uncertain but figured it would be okay if Dad was next to me. The camera was turned on and we took our seats in the last car.

The coaster clicked along, and I remember that it took an uncomfortably long time for the car to reach the top. It seemed like we were a mile above the planet. The view was spectacular, but I harbored little appreciation of it. My mind was filled with thoughts of dying and how much pain I was about to experience. I'm not sure what the voices in my head were saying, but I'm certain one of them was saying, "This is a bad idea. I could be home in bed right now!" Just as the first car disappeared, my father who had his arm draped over the back of the death car, simply said, "Nice knowin' you!" Nice knowing you? We're about to die the most painful and terrifying death imaginable, and that's all you have to say? Where is the DSS when you need them? "If I live through" this I thought, "I'm putting myself up for adoption!" We came down with the expected "Swish!" and a few minutes later the ride was over. I didn't see any of it as my eyes were closed so tight my forehead had cramps. I'm sure I left compression marks on the lap bar. I swore to myself that I would never ride another roller coaster again in my life. I've violated that promise dozens of times as the roller coaster somehow has become my favorite ride in any park.

The other time of note was when Dad asked me to go with him to a studio in Manhattan. Knowing no coasters were involved I said "Yes!" and off we went. A motion picture studio is an amazing place, especially to a young boy. There are all kinds of lights, cables, and cameras. Dad even took me up to the "Catwalk" which gave me a great view of the studio, even though we never came across any cats.

The movie Dad was working on was called, *Santa Clause Conquers the Martians*. It's rated as one of the top ten worst movies of all time and after seeing it, I had to agree with the evaluation of the critics. Of course, my father had nothing to do with the writing or performing, he just did his job and got paid. I didn't care either, because all I knew was that between takes, I was turned loose to jump into the spaceship. This thing had more buttons, levers, wheels, and gadgets than any little boy's imagination could conjure up. In my mind, I flew that spacecraft to the Moon, Mars, and Pluto. I even buzzed our house and saw my Mom in the backyard waving. I'm not sure what the men on the set thought as I bounced around that masterpiece of engineering, but believe me, I didn't care. I was captain of the greatest spaceship ever built. Up to that point, it was clearly the greatest day of my life!

Pearl River was blessed to have two theatres. The central theatre was near the old high school and the Pearl River theatre was in the center of town. Every once in a while, our parents would slide us a few coins and a Saturday afternoon would find a bunch of us making our way to the movies. The challenge was always to try to fool the person at the ticket booth about our age so we could get in for the children's price of 75 cents. If they didn't buy it, we would have to fork out the unheard-of price of $1.25.

Occasionally a couple of our friends couldn't come up with the price of a ticket even at the reduced rate. That was easily solved with a small strip of duct or masking tape. The ones who met the entrance fee, went in and found a seat. Then as soon as the previews started one of them would get up, crack the exit door open and tape the latch flat. Those outside, would keep trying the door until it opened. They would then slip in and enjoy the show.

A couple of my older peers found a very imaginative though dishonest, way of enjoying free entertainment. Without enough money to buy tickets they had to create a more inventive way of making up for their deficit. So, when there were two show times in the afternoon, they would show up at the theatre when the first show was nearing its end. Their entry ticket came in the form of an apple, orange, and at times, a tennis ball. They would select a car on the side street that they reasoned belonged to a movie-goer. The obstruction was inserted in the tailpipe, and they waited for the show to be over.

When the owner came out, he would find that his car wouldn't start. One of the guys would approach the car and ask what was wrong. He would explain that his Dad or uncle was a mechanic and that he wanted to look at the engine. While the hood was being lifted, the other guy would wander behind the car and clear the exhaust. The culprit in the front would move some wires and explain that the problem was fixed. Of course, the engine started right up. The driver was usually so thankful for the "expert" help from a "fine young man" and usually reward him with a dollar or two. Moments later the boys were seated in front of the screen with a box of popcorn and a drink.

-4-
THE MAGIC WORLD OF WATER

Dad got the idea that we should have a pool. I don't remember us begging for one. He just came up with the idea himself. He did that a lot. Decades before the creation of social media, he learned that a family was selling their redwood pool and he bought it. We took the pool apart and reassembled it at our place. The pool was a rectangle in shape with a deck and railing going all the way around. For nighttime swimming, Dad mounted several kerosene torches on poles around the rails. Games like dodgeball, *Marco Polo*, volleyball, tag, and the creation of amazing whirlpools were in abundance. Hours of pool activity were engaged in from late spring to early fall.

During one season, we actually had to rebuild the pool after a large pile of carpenter ants had their way. I remember sitting at the kitchen table with Mom when we heard a hollow thud. We looked out the back door just in time to see the last of the water leave the back corner of the pool. The water gushed into the street and left a dark water mark halfway across Manor Blvd. Before too long, Dad had ordered another liner and plywood and we were building the pool again. In short order we were back in action.

Before we had a pool, Nanuet Lake was the source of our reprieve from the summer heat. Sometime during the week, it was announced that we would be going to the lake on Saturday. Mom packed a mountain of food and around 10 o'clock all eight of us jumped in the station wagon and headed down the road for the day. To my young eyes, the lake seemed gigantic. There was a kiddie area roped off for wading, a raft in the middle, a dam at the far end, and a diving board. The pipe in the corner of the shallow pool pumped in ice cold water. The challenge was always to see how long you could hold your head under the water before the *brain freeze* forced you out. Near the kiddie pool was a complete refreshment stand filled with ice cream and other snacks. The lake was lined with picnic tables as well as a walking trail and areas for horseshoes. We normally claimed the same table each week, so we got to know those on either side of us.

Dad's rule was that none of us could go past the rope into the deep end until we could swim across the lake. It was probably only one hundred yards, but my mind held it as a mile. I had taken swim lessons at the lake and the day finally came when I would make my attempt to cross *the ocean* and gain the privilege of free entrance to the deep water. I told Dad that I was going to do it and launched myself from the far end toward our family's table. Before long, my head felt like it was in a washing machine. I did my best not to panic but was filled with doubt shortly after passing the half-way point. I pressed on and reached the other side gaining my newly earned freedom. My father had gotten involved in conversation and when I told him what I had done, and he told me that he didn't see it. My heart sank! I had risked my life and had what had to be a near-death experience and he missed it? Is there any fairness to this life? Fortunately, Dot had seen me and came to my rescue. Dad took her word for it and within minutes the danger I had just faced was forgotten and I was jumping off the raft in the middle of the lake.

When we weren't in the pool or at the lake, there were tons of other place we would go to enjoy water life. The nearby reservoir provided one of those places. Along Sickletown Road was a popular (and illegal) place to swim. By cutting through the cemetery, you would come to a large tree on the hill next to the water. A rope was hanging from a branch, allowing one to swing way out into the water. The place was called "Neal's." Word had it that it was named after a kid who failed to let go of the rope, came back, and hit the tree and drowned. Lots of kids congregated there and unofficially looked out for each other. We also looked out for the police. Invariably the cry, "Cheese it the cops!" was called out and in short order the place was as vacant as a schoolhouse on a Sunday afternoon.

The day of the senior prom meant the girls were skipping school to pick up their prom dresses and get their hair done. For us guys, it meant, well, it meant nothing other than we needed to skip school as well. Wayne, Wally, and I found ourselves at the reservoir near the Little League field. We swam out to the middle and were jumping off the electrical tower—that's right *electrical*—smart, I know. While sunning on the shore, we were approached by someone we didn't want to see. There was no "Cheese it-the cops!" cry so we were trapped. Truancy and trespassing were sure to get us a free ride in a police car. We could see the girls' mascara running. But he gave us a lecture and let us go! There really is a God!

As was mentioned earlier, the *40 Foot Hole* was a favorite haunt. It's a place where the Hackensack River emptied into the reservoir (Lake Tappan). The bridge was made of oversized stones fitted to make a large arch. It was a place of great entertainment all my growing up years. Besides catching so many wild animals and fish we launched plenty of rocks off the top of the bridge simply for the splash effect. One time, we even dumped over a railroad tie certain that it broke the splash record.

Often, when we caught a Bullfrog or two, we would deliver them to Deedee's on the way home. Deedee owned a bar, which was on Ehrhardt road, about a half mile from home. He had a hunched back and so we always referred to him as "DeeDee the hunchback." We never meant anything derogatory by it. It was just said to identify whom we were talking about. Of course, he was the only DeeDee we knew, and we could have called him "DeeDee the bar owner" but I guess it didn't have as much appeal to us. DeeDee would buy the frogs for .25 a piece and then cook frog's legs for one of his patrons. A quarter is not much but it was enough to buy five Hershey bars from Brushes deli on Middletown Road and Lang Terrace.

In Nauraushaun, one of the small tributaries of Lake Tappan flowed by a place aptly named *Silver Rocks*. It is so named because there were giant rocks painted silver that lined the edge of the road. A few of them are still there today. Plenty of fish, turtles, snakes, and crawfish could be found in the shallow stream. While fishing there one day in sixth grade, Casey, Franky, and I met a few older kids from a nearby school. We talked for a while, then left them to head down the road to Van Houten Farm and store to get a soda. We left our poles there with our lines in the water, pooled our money, and headed down toward our point of refreshment.

Van Houten Farms was just that. It was a store that carried everything needed to stock your kitchen with a plethora of vegetables. In the winter, it boasted a large Santa Clause or Snowman out front. In the Spring, a huge rabbit was on display. In the fall, a gigantic witch in front of a cauldron was in place. The witch brought fear and fascination to any young eyes which fell on her.

We made our way back from Van Houten's to find the other kids gone and my pole missing. I swore revenge! They were nowhere to be seen. I happened to glance down and see my pole in about three free of water. They had tossed it in, heightening my desire for revenge. I waded into the water and grabbed my pole. I was determined to find those guys and tear into them. When I pulled on my pole it pulled back. On the end of my line, I found the largest catfish I had ever laid eyes on. To this day, I'm not sure I caught anything bigger. Those boys were quickly pardoned, and we celebrated the big catch before letting him go with hopes that we'd meet again.

Mom informed Dad on more than one occasion that she wanted a boat. Finally, Dad capitulated and brought home a boat. We were the proud owners of a Grumman aluminum seventeen-foot canoe! That canoe provided hours of fun and adventure! Except for a few camping trips Dad took us on, for the most part we spent our *Boat Life* on the Hackensack River. When we asked far enough in advance, I'm not sure if Dad ever said "No" to a trip down the Hackensack. It was on that very river that I learned so many boating skills which I carry with me today. After we got older, we were able to sequester the boat ourselves and get dropped off with the vessel. Most of the time, we would put in at Route 59 and take out at the *40-Foot Hole*. This meant that we traveled about five miles in search of wildlife, fun, and adventures to build years of memories.

After a very heavy rain fall at age twelve, Franky and I persuaded my father to let us take the canoe down the river. We were sure the flow of the river would be fast with a promise of a great ride. So, we loaded the boat in the station wagon and headed out for what we knew would be an unusually fast trip. We stopped about the half-way point at the Deer Head Inn and surveyed the river. It was immensely swollen and flowing faster than we had imagined. The water was so high that it was popping up against the girders of the bridge making the bridge impassable by water. The far side of the bank met with a steep incline which could not be scaled from the boat. We were ordered to hug the near bank and get out a good distance before the bridge. With strict instruction from my father about portaging across the road, we headed for our input point on Route 59. I won the rear seat which meant that I was responsible for steering.

The flow of the river did not disappoint. In minutes we were in sight of the turn in the river and heading for the portage point. As we rounded the turn, I glanced up to see my father on the bridge. He may have been yelling instructions, but the noise of the water was too great for us to hear. The river was moving so quickly that the current pushed us to the far side—the wrong side! We fought hard to cross the stream with the bridge getting ever closer. About twenty yards from the bridge, we managed to wedge the nose of the boat between two trees. Franky grabbed the trees and held the front of the boat between them. At this point, the canoe was perpendicular to the river. But the current was so strong that it began to bend the boat and fill it with water. I yelled for Franky to let go and get out. He jumped out and I began to spin with the boat toward the bridge. I dove for the shore and managed to catch some brush and the tops of small trees. I reached for the limb of a dead tree and felt the current pulling at my legs. Seconds later the branch snapped, and I was headed once again for the bridge. By swimming with everything I had and grabbing at anything I could find, I pulled hard and was able to get to the shore and join Franky and my father. With a sick feeling in our guts, we could hear the canoe as it tumbled under the bridge hitting every beam along the way. Recounting that story, I remember my Dad telling me that he had never been so scared in his life. I related very well to that emotion.

After drying off and warming up, we were back on the river below the bride with a borrowed canoe searching for our boat. We found it in short order, pressed by the current against the bank.

One day my mother reminded my father that when she said she wanted a boat she meant one she didn't have to paddle. Dad took it to heart and shortly arrived home with a fourteen foot "Sunfish" sailboat. I can still see my Mom shaking her head and giving a "What am I gonna do with you?" sigh. Nevertheless, that boat provided lots of fun for the whole family. It had a shallow cockpit for our feet, and plenty of deck room for our hind parts. The boat is rated for two people, but we normally had four of us on it at a time.

When Dad felt we were old enough, he released the boat to us to skim the surface of Lake Tiorati (Seven Lakes Drive). But for the most part we spent our time plunging the waters of the mighty Hudson River. Mom would pack a big lunch (as always) and we would head out to a spot in Stony Point. The place we chose had piles of smooth glass lying all around. The edges of all the glass had been worn off by the water and posed no danger. We nicknamed the place, "Glass Beach." All of us, including Dad, learned our sailing skills during those great trips.

The first time we took the boat out was a memorable one. None of us could wait for great weather so we went out on a day before the temperatures got very comfortable. John, Jeff, Dad, and I all mounted the vessel and took off for some time on the river. My Dad explained so much about sailing which I'm sure he learned mostly from reading. One of the big terms I learned was, "Coming About." That means that you're turning around. There are two ways to turn a sailing vessel. You can turn into the wind, which is more of a gentle turn, or you can turn away from the wind, which means the wind catches the back end of the sail first and pops it full. When you opt for the latter move, the key is to let the sail out, so you don't have as much resistance to the wind. On our first turn, we came about away from the wind. When my Dad went to let the sail out, someone was sitting on the rope—yes, it was me! The sail stayed tight, the wind caught it, and over we went! Our first trip in the sailboat and we capsized!

Most times, when it was just Dad with a couple of us kids, we would stop by a beverage store in Bardonia and get a case of soda. Dad always had to have crème soda! We'd put that case in the cockpit, rest our feet on it, and spend the day on the Hudson.

We had so many great times in that boat. We criss-crossed the Hudson more times than we could count and built memories with every wave and gust of wind.

Occasionally I would be invited by some friends to join their family for a trip to the Jersey shore. Because of the proximity to the

New Jersey Turnpike, a day trip to the beach could be easily managed. Seaside Heights, Barnegat Light House, Point Pleasant, and Cape May were all common favorites. The day was filled from end to end with activity. Swimming, board riding, tossing a football, fishing, and exploring the boardwalk were all part of the day. One time, we presented Ricky and Stanly's Dad with a gift to be enjoyed when we got home. We had been down by the inlet checking things out. We came across a few crab traps and quickly pulled them up. In minutes we were proud possessors of a half dozen crabs. We didn't know it was illegal and got a gentle lecture for our efforts. The crabs were turned loose, and we were too.

-5-

THE WINTER WONDERLAND

Somehow it seemed to snow more back in my days of boyhood. This gave us hours of adventure and a few dollars made from shoveling sidewalks and driveways. I remember waking up on several mornings and seeing a note in front of my desk clock, "No school today. Go back to sleep." I tried. I really tried. But I had ruined my chances of slumbering by looking out the window and catching a glimpse of the snow-covered earth. Before long, I was fully insulated and heading down the street with a snow shovel resting on my shoulder. You had to hustle and get the driveway done before the snowplow came by and undid some of your work. I cleared several driveways and sidewalks in the next two hours. Arriving home, warm and satisfied with a good bit of money in my pocket, I headed straight for the kitchen. Mom made a meal of tomato soup and grilled cheese. Then I slept for an hour and was back in the snow with my neighborhood buddies. Snowball fights, snow forts, and record-breaking snowmen came in a flurry. Many days ended with us rolling as big a snowball as we could and pushing it to the center of Ehrhardt road forcing cars to drive around it. Irritating behavior cannot be frozen!

Sleigh riding was big in those days. Blue Hill golf course provided the downhill we needed for thrills and spills and the place was always crowded with families enjoying their rides. There was one area of the course that held a particular attraction. It was called "Suicide Hill." It was by far the steepest hill I had ever sledded on. It seemed more like a cliff than a hill. It was so dangerous that after a period of time and several injuries, it was closed to sledding. The bottom held a sand trap that ended in a jump that sent any rider airborne concluding the ride. When you hit the bump, you crashed. If you somehow missed the ramp you headed for the road. Still, it was a place for daring and double daring. After it was closed to sledding if you got caught, the police would escort you off the property.

In middle school I was with some friends on the *legal* part of the course. We made several runs when my friend John was plowed into by a sled. The front of the sled hit him in the shin, and he went flying. We laughed and then helped put him back together. On Monday at school, we made fun of his limp—that's what you did in those days. The next day we were surprised to see him arrive at school on crutches and wearing a cast. Our sorrow for him may have lasted an hour.

The property of Lederle Laboratories provided another place to sled. The walk from our house was about half a mile, but the thrills and spills to be had were enough to motivate us to drag our sleds and toboggan that far. Before the highway (Route 304) was built, there was a long and steep run on the edge of some woods. This place too was crowded with young life. Someone got the idea of making a ramp from the hood of an old Buick pulled from the woods. We kept replacing the snow on it but there were always some sparks that flew from the rails of our sleds. It was a glorious sight and brought lots of cheers. On one run, Pat hit the ramp and went airborne. When he hit the ground, he split his sled down the middle making his body a snowplow with his face in the lead.

During one large snow, my Dad decided he would help us build a snow fort. Typical of my Dad, nothing was ever done halfway. We wouldn't be building just any snow fort. We would be building a full-sized igloo. He gave instructions and worked side-by-side with us and before long, we had a beautiful igloo complete with a tunnel for an entrance. We even put marks in the surface, so it looked like it had been cut out of chunks of snow. But that was not enough. Dad pulled the hose from the garage and sent a mist over our creation ensuring that it would last for several days of the ensuing warmer climate. A blanket on the floor and hot chocolate in our bellies made for hours of relaxation and fun.

Naturally, driving in the snow was a treat. The high school parking lot served as a place to do "patch outs" and "donuts." During school one day, it began to snow lightly. The school district was deciding whether to release us early. I was sitting in biology class spending more time looking outside than listening to what was going on inside when I saw the car of a state trooper pull up. Out popped my friend Bill. He was caught doing "donuts" on the Palisades Parkway and was summarily escorted back to school.

One evening, during a particularly heavy snowstorm I endeavored to drive to my girlfriend Diane's house. I borrowed my Mom's car and made it as far as the base of the hill on Central Avenue. I tried a couple of times to climb the hill but wound up sliding backwards almost down to Rt. 304. While I weighed my options, a car came over the hill and went sliding into 304 traffic. The police were called and arrived also at the top of the hill. I watched two police cars come past me and become part of the accident they were investigating. At the top of the hill another police car stopped and parked. The officer got out and tried to walk down the ice clad hill. Hard leather shoes are no match for ice! He went about three steps and began his slide. He too went past me but on his back. I know it wasn't right, but laughter was my dominant emotion.

A classmate of Dot's named Bruce made mental headlines when he decided the snow-covered steps leading to the school courtyard would be a great place to drive. He made it down with no trouble circling the courtyard once. The return became problematic. Visions of Dean Satz (we called him "Lumpy" behind his back) banging on his door still flow through my mind and bring a chuckle to my heart.

Behind St. Aedan's Catholic Church was a moderately sized pond. During the summer this served as a great place for fishing, catching turtles, and hunting for snakes. But in the winter, this was to be a place for everything an ice surface could bring. For several years, somewhere around Thanksgiving it became the unofficial duty of Glenn to stop up the drainpipes when a storm was brewing. Mother Nature did her job in supplying the natural water and a hose from the church supplied the rest. Before anyone knew what we had done (and turned off the water), The pond swelled to what must have been a two-acre center of activity. We had an area marked off for hockey, a free skate area, and a multitude of trails through the swamp. It was not uncommon for us to form a "Whip." This doesn't seem like much to turn your head, but when you're at the end of a twenty-five-person line, it has all your attention.

The light from the parking lot and the brightness of fresh snow allowed us to skate late into the night. Often, we would scramble home to pick up the assigned ingredients to cook potato slices in a pan over an open fire. There's just something magical about standing around a fire holding a paper plate of freshly cooked potato slices.

-6-
TALKING SMACK

Communication is part of life. It's how we get along and go along. But learning to communicate creatively adds color to everything we say. It's the fizz in our drinks and the spice to our food. As a young Pearl Riverite, learning to talk effectively and sometimes cruelly were all part of those growing up years.

A few years back, when our boys were about in middle school or early high school, they introduced me to their version of put downs. It went something like this:

> "Can you pass me the salt?"
> "I'll show you the salt!"
> "Really? That's it?"

> "Give me a glass."
> "You're a glass!"
> Again, "Really? That's all you've got?"

This is what parents call a teachable moment. I explained to them that their version of a put down would have to improve to reach the level of lame. Come backs usually fell into the categories of insults and threats.

I told them that a real put down needs to be visionary and creative.

A few of the ones we employed went something like this:

"You're so ugly, when you were born, the doctor slapped your mother!"

"You got a haircut? It's amazing what the blind can do!"

"That teacher's so fat she leaves stretch marks in the bathtub."

"Your sister's so skinny she's gotta run around in the shower to get wet."

"If my dog was as ugly as you, I'd shave his butt and teach him to walk backward!"

"You lost weight? Look under your shirt and you'll find it."

"I'm gonna beat you like a rented mule."

"I used to have a shirt like that but then my father got a job."

"Is that your face or did your neck throw-up?"

And my personal favorite,

"I'm gonna kick you so hard in the groin, your kids are gonna be born with shoe polish on their heads."

Sometimes these insults and threats would lead to a fight but most often they ended in laughter, slight embarrassment, and a commitment to come up with your own insult or threat. Our skin was a good bit tougher back then. Today, these comments might win you an appointment in a courtroom and public condemnation because "Someone's feelings were hurt."

-7-
TRAGEDY OF THE HEART

I was only ten years old, but I could sense the grief and loss that rocked our small town. On May 10th 1967, at the age of twenty-three, Heintz Ahlmeyer was struck down while serving in Viet Nam. He was the first person from our town that died in the war. Later, Robert Bauer (age 23) and Robert Kernan (age 21) would also die in the war.

In that same year, football co-captain, Brian Armstrong would die from a brain stem injury suffered during a Saturday afternoon football game. The Pirates were playing the Clarkstown Rams when Brian was injured in the third quarter. He died the following Wednesday at the age of seventeen. The athletic department still gives out "The Brian Armstrong" scholarship to the best football player each season. Though I was young, I knew anyone who died playing the game I loved deserved my honor and respect.

In January of our junior year, tragedy came closer to home. On January 2nd, the ambulance pulled up to the parking lot next to the gym. The entire school was astir. Brian Elliott, one of our classmates was loaded on a stretcher and whisked away. Brian had been feeling poorly but still dressed out for Physical Education class. He was doing a muscle up on the rings, came down to the floor and passed out. Another classmate, Chuck came to help. Due to double pneumonia, Brian had stopped breathing. Chuck was trained and administered CPR while the rescue crew was called. Somewhere between the gym floor and the hospital, my friend passed away. That was the day I learned that death is no respecter of persons.

-8-
CONTINUED ADVENTURES

One Sunday afternoon our family along with several others were invited to a party at the home of some family friends. There were plenty of kids and adults, so the energy was high. It didn't take long for us kids to find an adventure in the back yard. At the crest of a good-sized hill in the back yard was a huge rock. The end of the property butted up against the dead-end road of a neighborhood. An apartment complex was being constructed on the right side of the property at the bottom of the hill.

We decided that it would be fun and exciting to dig out the lower end of the dirt and send the giant boulder down the hill and into the street. If we could move the beast, it would be monumental—one for the record books. With sticks and our hands, we began digging taking turns pulling out the dirt. We never considered the danger of the rock rolling onto one of us, but death was sure to pay a visit. This was added to a long and growing list of things we never considered during childhood.

In the middle of our foolish project my father and a few of the other men came out to check on us. When Dad saw what we were doing he scolded us. "You dumb kids have no idea what you're doing!" And he was right! But then these unforgettable words jumped from his mouth. "You need leverage! Now grab that 2x6 and bring over that cinder block." This was my father speaking. Dad—the compliant and strict one! We scrambled and brought the implements. After a quick lesson on leverage and fulcrums, Dad and the men began to lean on the board. I can still feel the excitement in my gut. The rock began to move and then slowly, very slowly it tilted and started down the hill. We cheered.

But then the amazing and unthinkable thing happened. The mammoth rock hit something—another rock or a large root perhaps. But it changed the direction of the beast. The rock made a forty-five-degree shift, went through some small bushes, and crashed through the wall of the apartment complex. The echo of the collision must have been heard for blocks. Everyone stood there motionless, taking in what had just happened. The silence was broken by another unforgettable word from my father, "Run!" For the remainder of the day, the party continued inside the house and on the front lawn with only whispers detailing the previous episode.

-9-
THE DEALS WITH WHEELS

Creativity, ingenuity, and resourcefulness brought America the car. These same qualities brought us mobility as well. But when motors were not available from neighboring garbage piles, we counted on gravity to move us. We made Go-Karts from planks of wood and baby carriage wheels. We would use one 2x6 board and loosely bolt a 2x4 to the front. Another 2x4 was secured to the back. Two wheels were attached to each 2x4, and ropes were tied to the front enabling us to steer. If we got lucky, we would find a plastic chair and remove the legs. This served as our driver's seat. We always left room behind the seat for a passenger. The break was simply a stick of wood that was nailed to the side within arm's reach. By pulling on the stick and putting your feet down, you could stop relatively quickly.

An unforgettable event took place on the hill of Manor Blvd. We were in the area where they were building new homes. They had laid the initial asphalt down and it made for great riding. I was there one day with my friend David. We made a couple of trips down the hill and hauled our vehicle back up by the steering rope. On a memorable trip down, I was driving, and David was standing on the back holding on to the back of the seat. One wheel caught the edge of a dip in the road and the Go-Kart turned sideways. I was spilled out of the Kart and David came down on the back of my head. At first, I just felt the burn of my arms and face sliding along the asphalt. Then my tongue revealed to me that I had broken one of my front teeth. I still have a cap and a painful memory of that day.

Skates with wooden wheels were only used at the indoor skating rink. For outdoor use, roller skates were metal and made for the road and sidewalk. They had adjustable clips in the front and a leather strap to go over the ankle keeping them in place. Each set of skates came with a key to adjust the clamp at the front of the sneakers. By attaching a rope to the back of a bike we could be towed at dangerous speeds. It was a thrilling ride until you hit a crack or stone in the road. At that point the only enjoyment was had by our friends who were spectators of the fall.

Along with building wooden Go-Karts, we made stand up scooters. Again, we'd use a good length of 2x6 for a base. Then we'd split one of our metal roller skates and attach each end to the bottom of the board. A quip trip to the local supermarket and some begging secured us a vegetable crate. The crate was stood on end and nailed to the 2x6. A short length of a narrow board was nailed to the top of the crate giving us a stand-up scooter that rolled easily down the street.

On our bikes we traveled wherever our hearts would lead us. We never worried about traffic or how far away a destination was. If we decided on a place to go, we just hopped on our bikes and headed out. By the time I was in sixth grade I had traveled as far as Lake Welch (twenty miles) and the big golf ball on the hill in Orangeburg on the other side of Route 303.

Our bank accounts never allowed for a ten speed, and we never spent much time dreaming about it. We just took off on our one-speed and zig-zagged up and sped down the hills of the town. Helmets were equally unheard of then. It would have taken too much time to strap them on and who knows what we would have missed and how much ribbing we would have to endure. A Schwinn was the bike to have, and Billy was blessed to have one with a *banana seat*. Besides being stylish, this meant that he was able to carry someone else with him without them having to ride on the handlebars or sidesaddle on the bruising cross bar.

It was while riding sidesaddle on my brother John's bike that we crashed. We were going down Lang Terrace, also known as "Snaky Hill." We had a full head of steam when somehow my foot floated to the right and got caught in the front spokes. In seconds we were airborne. I landed in some bushes on someone's front yard and

John landed in the street. The ambulance was called for John who suffered a sprained wrist, plenty of abrasions, and multiple contusions. I limped away from the scene with only a bruised foot and the guilt of having caused the accident.

Every once in a while, when we wanted our "Badness" to go all the way to the bone, we would take clothespins and pin a couple of baseball cards on the supports on the wheels of our bikes. The spokes would rake across the cards and with a little imagination, make our bikes sound just like motorcycles. When we wore the cards out, we simply replaced them with more cards.

Jumping our bikes was a lot of fun as well. We'd take a brick or cinder block, lean a short piece of plywood against it, and be all set to compete for distance. Coming down the hill added both distance and danger to this activity.

When building the parking lot at St. Aedan's Catholic church, several mounds of cinders were placed in different piles around the lot. The temptation was too great. Before long, we had a patted down area to get some speed up before hitting the four-foot-high mound. It was challenging but wonderful! Each time I rode, I picked up more and more speed and went higher and higher. I would be flying and land professional-like on my back tire. After a few "record-setting jumps," my back tire gave out and went flat. What was I to do? It was too good of a time to just walk away. The only solution? Go and get my sister Dot's bike.

In very short order I was back with her bike and sitting on the edge of the parking lot waiting for my turn to fly. I came down the trail, hit the hill with everything I had, and was sailing toward the clouds, when...the front wheel came off! I watched the wheel go free of the bike and held my position to land on the back tire. This solved nothing! The back tire landed as it should and then the front forks buried themselves in the ground. I went flying over the handlebars and felt the intense and indescribable burning sensation as the skin was torn from both my arms, my short-clad thighs, and the left side of my face. I checked my teeth and found them in place but knew I was going to be a long time in scabbing over. I'm certain that I had my tire fixed and I was out riding again within a couple of days.

Matt proved to be one of the best tire rollers in the group. Just for the fun of it, we would roll a tire down Manor Boulevard to see who could roll it the farthest. We took turns retrieving the tire for another roll. As things go, this game evolved into another less innocent (and less legal) one.

Lang Terrace ended at Manor Boulevard. This took place at the bottom of the hill a hundred yards from where Manor Boulevard joined Ehrhardt Road. By noting the directional signal letting us know a car was turning left, we signaled Matt to let the tire go. The timing was remarkably accurate. As a car slowed down to make a left turn, "Bamm!" the tire would crash against the side wall making a very loud sound. The driver never saw it coming and because the tire fell on its side, they didn't know what hit them. Matt disappeared safely into the bushes as soon as he let the tire go. We were already securely hidden away leaving the driver deeply puzzled and angry. Matt did several rolls before the police caused a panicked scattering and threw a wet blanket on our destructive time of play.

-10-
LIFE IN THE WOODS

My buddies and I didn't own the woods, but you would never know it by the way we carried on there. It was in the woods that we built a deluxe tree fort. Permanently barrowing wood from a neighborhood housing development, we marched proudly down the road on a Sunday afternoon—when no one was working—Into the woods with everything needed to build our fortress. When my father learned what we were doing, he jumped in to secure the boards to the trees. He knew we were inexperienced—which is a kind word for stupid, so he wanted to make sure we were safe. Then he slipped away and let the young engineers go to work. When we were done, we had constructed a two-story fort compete with a 2x4 ladder, upper floor trap door, and a zip-line for excitement and easy escape from evil pursuers.

The zip line was an after-thought but one that gave us hours of thrills and entertainment. To construct the zipline we ran a long rope from the top floor of our castle to a large tree about one hundred feet away. We tied the rope to the trees but secured them with nails—can't be too careful! We had a long line on the pulley so we could run it back to the next flyer. I don't remember who went first, but we quickly learned that the undergrowth was pulling on the line and interfering with a smooth ride. So, we mustered some tools from our homes and went to work eliminating the problem.

Because we were young and lacked the strength needed to cut the growth at the base, we cut the small trees as far down as we could. Before long we had cut a six-foot swath the length of the course. This meant that we had a one hundred-foot-long row of vertical knives coming from the ground—I still don't understand how we lived through those days.

After a period of climbing up to the fort we somehow decided to go down. We were going to dig an underground fort. Gathering digging tools from home, we found a spot we reasoned would be ideal. Then we went to work. We dug a hole about four-feet deep and six feet square. Next, we made a three-foot trench to serve as an entrance. Then, after *borrowing* some more lumber from the housing development, we placed 2x6s in grooves along the top edge. We covered that with plywood and finished with a load of dirt and some plants. We had an underground fort, complete with a ledge to sit on and candles to light the room.

One day when we were being chased by someone, which was always the goal, we reached the woods and headed to the safety of the fort. Seconds after we arrived, Bill and I chickened out and ran by the entrance. We reasoned that the fort might be safe but might also trap us with no escape. So, we dove behind some bushes to ensure a better getaway. My brother Casey however, dove into the opening without hesitation. From the safety of some bushes, Bill and I watched as the *enemy* paced back and forth over the top of Casey's head.

On another day we decided to play *Vietnam*. Growing up, all our military enemies were either labeled Germans (Krauts), or Viet Cong. The three of us rushed home to get our BB guns—I know, you'll shoot your eye out! One guy was to go ahead and lay "the ambush." Our task was to get from one end of the woods to the other without getting shot by the VC. On this day, Billy was the enemy, and Casey and I were the Green Beret. Knowing we were in enemy territory put us on high alert. Then the ambush started. The first BB hit Casey in the leg, and he screamed and jumped behind a tree. We identified where Billy was and returned fire. Billy's gun had a scope making him much more accurate than us. I was convinced of this when I leaned from behind a tree and was shot in my bicep muscle way to close to my eye. A retreat ensued, the war ended, and all body parts were still intact albeit some of them were sore.

-11-
MIDDLE SCHOOL DAZE

Everyone at some point in their lives drives through *The Stupid Zone*. That is the place where you act without thinking. Consequences are not considered, and emotions rule the day and drive the choices.

In middle school I was *parked* in *The Stupid Zone*. Perhaps it was my need to be accepted and seeking to find my own identity. I'm not blaming any of my decisions on anyone. I made all my own choices. But I began to run with "the wrong crowd." Fighting, stealing, lying, vandalizing, and disrupting class became part of my middle school experience.

Each day during the announcements, the speakers in each room would play the song *Put a Little Love in Your Heart*. At least for me, it didn't work. I came to hate the song and not much love was found in my heart.

Part way through sixth grade I came to the misguided conclusion that it would be cool to start smoking. Several of my buddies smoked so I decided that it was time for me to join them. I bummed two cigarettes and puffed away. Before I finished the second one, I almost choked to death and vomited up a lung. I downplayed the whole thing and decided that smoking was not for me. This was one of the few smart choices I made while meandering through middle school.

By seventh grade I became such a nuisance that the principal threatened to put my name on a chair in the office. In Mr. Nelson's shop class, I got hold of some pieces of copper sheets. I took the tin snips and made my own set of "Ninja Stars." I couldn't wait to see how they worked. Again, without thinking, I threw one of my stars into the crowded hallway. It just missed a girl's head before imbedding into a bulletin board. Those who saw me do it never spoke up, so I didn't get caught.

To this day, I carry a small amount of guilt for the torment I put Mrs. Guttman through. She was the English teacher and was the brunt of most of my friends, and especially my, misbehavior. Several times she abandoned the class and hurried down the hall in tears. She just didn't know what to do with such a group of rebellious kids. I learned later that she was also struggling her way through some personal problems.

I got into a few fights with some kids from Nanuet and decided that it would be best if I carried a knife. I bought a six-inch leopard stiletto from Freddie and kept it neatly tucked in my back pocket. It was sleek and black with a beautiful leopard (hence the name) painted on the side. I practiced pulling it out and with a flick of my wrist could have the blade out and in the ready position. There were a couple of times when I almost used it, but thankfully it never came to that. There is no question that some decisions can be life altering.

While in shop class, I was being annoyed by a classmate named Tommy. I asked him if he wanted a punch in the face and he said "Yes," daring me to do it. He never backed down, so I repeated my offer. Again, he said, "Yes." With a haymaker to the side of his face I laid him out. Before he got up, Mr. Nelson was there to break things up. After class, I knew Tommy would be waiting for me after class, so I waited until everyone was out the door then exited in a low position. Sure enough, he swung at me. He barely hit me, and I caught him with my shoulder and pushed him into the stairwell. Again, the conflict was quickly over.

For no discernable reason I threw a garbage can out the second story window of Mrs. Guttman's class. I got caught and after school the principal gave me a garbage bag, pointed me outside and told me I couldn't leave school until the bag was full of garbage. I immediately went back inside, emptied three of the garbage cans from the classrooms, dropped the full bag off at the office—without seeing the principal, and made my bus.

The height of stupidity was seen in our decision to jump off the school patio. At the back of the school was an elevated patio. It was about fifteen feet off the ground and had a railing running all around the top. I don't know who the first person was but one of us answered the challenge to hang down from the railing and jump. Because he lived through it more and more of us joined in the experience. It became a post-phys. Ed. tradition and a mild rite of passage to jump. Wanting to be part of the group, and not being gifted with good judgment, I personally jumped several times. Some kids did get hurt and I remember one student broke his leg but that didn't seem to slow us down. This lunacy eventually died out and we moved on to other foolish endeavors.

One day, I was so disruptive on the bus that the driver threw me off. She tried to push me down the steps and without hesitating I pushed her down on the floor. I don't know why I wasn't suspended, but I was banned from the bus for the rest of the year. I solved that problem by taking another bus that picked me up and dropped me off a couple of blocks from my former stop.

Detention became a way of life and I got used to walking home from school. At one point, the teachers decided to hold an intervention. I was held after school as usual and led into a room. Chairs were formed a circle with one chair in the middle. It doesn't take a genius to guess where I was seated. One after another they pummeled me with threats and accusations. I can't claim that my behavior changed for more than a week. Somehow, I reasoned that the possibility of being accepted, admired, and noticed by my peers was greater than any threat the teachers could communicate or punishment they could deliver.

I'm not sure what my parents were thinking about all this. I'm certain they were tired of the phone calls and the details of my latest escapade. No amount of punishment had any lasting effect on me at school or at home. I was hell-bent on doing my own thing without hesitation or thoughts regarding the consequences.

One day an episode happened that led to my suspension. It was one of those rare times that I really wasn't guilty. But I lied about being there and so it was assumed that I was directly involved and was guilty. To be so young and to be so messed up is truly amazing. Even though I was young and foolish I could see that I was headed for deeper trouble and there had to be some changes.

Those changes came the summer between my seventh and eighth grade years. There was a movement that was prevalent in churches throughout our nation. Churches began to realize that for them to reach a future generation, they had to change the way they were reaching out to young people. With this idea in mind, "coffee houses" began to spring up in church basements and fellowship halls all around the country.

Rooms were painted loud colors and decorated with posters that glowed when the black lights were turned on. Music was live and more modern. Coffee and snacks were served, and testimonies were shared.

Down the street from our home was The Christian and Missionary Alliance church. I had gone there from time to time and as best as I can recall, enjoyed it each time. When I was younger, I even went to the Sunday School classes when the mood hit me. I don't know what drew me there but that summer I found myself going to the coffee house in the basement each Saturday night. I guess it gave me something to do and I enjoyed the music and atmosphere.

It was there that I first noticed "Church People" dressed in regular clothes. Beyond that, they were caring and accepting of me. It was also there that I saw the message of Christ lived out in people's lives. These guys were the "real deal!"

They told me about the sacrifice Jesus made for my sins, (and I knew there were enough to sink a battleship!) They explained to me what it meant to be forgiven of all the bad stuff that I had done and how just by praying I could become a Christian. After a while, it all sank in and began to make sense.

It was during this time that a particular Bible verse rose to the top of my mind and began to make sense. John 3:16, says, "For God so loved the world, that He gave His only begotten Son, that whosoever would believe in Him would not perish, but have everlasting life."

One of the older guys at the coffee house broke this verse down and brought it home to my heart by personalizing it. He said that God loves the entire world—every man, woman, and child, even Steve, so very much that He was willing to give His one and only unique Son so that whoever including Steve would really believe in

Him, he would have eternal life in heaven.

Wow! That verse hit me like a cold cup of water on a steamy Pearl River summer day. That was the love and acceptance that I wanted but could never find outside of my family. All the fighting, stealing, and carrying on couldn't bring the peace and acceptance I was looking for.

While at home that summer I knelt by a chair in an upstairs room and prayed. I asked Jesus Christ to forgive me for my sins and to come into my life and change me.

I didn't hear a booming voice and the stars didn't engage in a cooperative exercise to spell out my name, but I knew, I just knew that something had changed in me. I couldn't explain it but somehow, I knew I was a different person. I still had a bad reputation to deal with and plenty of opportunities to get into trouble, but I knew beyond a shadow of doubt that I would be okay. A peace came over me that has never left.

I'm ashamed to say that I kept that episode quiet. Somehow, I felt that if word got out, others would see it as weakness, and I would become the target of violence, abuse, and ridicule. So, I kept my newfound faith to myself and worked my way through the haze of those middle school days. I drifted away from the friends I had and began to attend church on Sundays. The rest of the week was spent doing what I had to get by socially and scholastically.

I'm disappointed to admit that this undercover life continued throughout my high school years. Most people came to see me as a nice guy and attributed it to my deeper involvement in sports. But I knew that the change in me was due to my relationship with Christ. It wasn't until I got to college that I became bold in my faith and was willing to share it and desired to really grow as a Christian.

As a high school freshman, I began to get a sense of growing into manhood. I took more responsibility at home and grew in my self-sufficiency. Although my brothers and sisters had curfews, I never had one. Discipline became the hallmark of my life and I worked, trained, and developed a routine that I felt comfortable in.

One night, my parents went out for the evening. I was home with my sisters, Casey, and one of his friends. During a heavy storm, the lights went out. We got out a couple of flashlights and some candles and sort of enjoyed the excitement of it all.

Then we heard a thumping in the basement. Immediately our minds raced to an incident that had recently happened in Long Island. While having coffee in the kitchen, two women heard a bumping coming from the dryer in the basement. One of the ladies got up and headed to her basement thinking there were shoes in the dryer. She began going down the stairs when she remembered that she hadn't been doing the laundry. She went back up and called the police. When they arrived, they found a convicted rapist standing there waiting for the woman to come down. He had entered from an outside door and was using the dryer to lure her down. The night of the storm brought that incident to the forefront of our minds, and we concluded, "The guys loose and he's in our basement! He got in through the storm door!"

As the non-rhythmical thumping continued, I decided I would go down and confront the criminal. I grabbed a large kitchen knife and a flashlight and head toward the stairs giving instructions that if I yelled, the others were to leave the house, go next door, and call the police.

In the basement, the thumping continued from the back room. I knew he was there, and I was poised to change his day. When I rounded the corner, my flashlight shined on a full-length mirror. All at once I sucked the air out of the entire room, as I simultaneously stabbed the mirror and fell backwards.

Quietly laughing, I gathered my wits and balance about me and moved toward the continued sound. I got closer and closer in the darkened room and mentally begged the convict to make his move. When I got close enough to the dryer, I saw the source of the thumping. The wind was blowing the dryer flap up and it was popping against the house. Again, I laughed nervously to (and at) myself. After a few minutes I went upstairs and reported most of the story to the others. The hero had returned! After a few weeks had past, I felt comfortable in telling them all the details of what really went on downstairs.

-12-
LIFE AS A PIRATE

High school was a blast, maybe too much of a blast. This is probably how I made the top half of the class possible and why I struggled so much in college to keep my head above water, at least above "C" level. (Pun intended!). I bounced from group to group feeling equally at home no matter where I was. I loved telling stories and enjoyed making people laugh—I still do!

At the time I came through the system, Pearl River high school carried a student body of 1,300 and I was one of a class of 313. In those days athletic conferences were not determined by school size. Conferences were defined by the county lines. We were the smallest school in Rockland County, but we held our own with every opponent we played in every sport.

It was in high school that I felt the pride I carried for the Pearl River Pirates rise to the top. I learned that there are many types of pride. There's personal pride, family pride, national pride, & Pirate pride. As a young boy, I loved hearing the drums and music from the band on Saturday mornings as they warmed up. It meant the Pirates would be playing football. I had little money, so I used to sneak into the games by climbing the fence on Pearl Crest Court. In middle school, some buddies and I would get into the game by waiting for the ticket taker to be distracted and then simply leaping over the snow fence.

I played football in middle school. Play was restricted to seventh and eighth graders. We had so many kids that wanted to play that we had four teams. It was an inter-squad program and you played against your classmates. The team colors were red, green, gold, and blue. The teams played each other a couple of times during the abbreviated season, and I really enjoyed being part of a team.

On the high school level, Pete Dyer was the varsity football coach. Before coming to P.R. he was well-known for his success at Dobbs Ferry on the other side of the Hudson River. He loved the New York Giants and as a result, our uniforms were patterned after them. Pete was not necessarily mechanical. None the less, his wife was repeatedly asking him to paint their bathroom. There is little time for such things during the season. But, to appease her, he painted their bathroom during half time of a Giant's game. It was not a job worth bragging about.

As a ninth grader, this would be the first time I would be under the coaching staff of Coach Dyer. After college graduation I got to coach with him and was later privileged to preach his funeral.

That first practice, we sat in the shade provided by the shadow of the gym. The varsity guys looked like giants and I was intimidated. Coach gave the team rules, and I took notes:

No smoking, no drinking, no drugs. I wasn't doing those things anyway but I wrote them down so I wouldn't forget and do them by mistake. Summers were hot and humid. We were on the field early in the morning and practiced twice a day. I still remember how uncomfortable it was to have my shorts soaked through by the damp grass. The usual shenanigans went on with someone invariably having to run inside because of the hot stuff that was spread in his jock. At other times, small stones would be bounced off helmets as we stretched and warmed up. This gave you a ringing in your head for about ten minutes.

There were several conditioning constants that were part of every practice:

Monkey Rolls: This involved three players lying on the ground and popping up and over the person next to him and rolling out of the way of the next guy. When it's done well and quickly it's actually quite invigorating. But somehow amid the heat and exhaustion you didn't feel that way.

Bull in the Ring: One player was placed in the center of a circle of players. When he turned and pointed at someone forming the circle, that person would rush him and slam against him trying to knock him off his feet. A sure way to thin out your squad through head injury or loss of will.

Cross-the-Bow Tackling: In this drill, one player assumes the role of the ball carrier. Another player runs to him putting his head and shoulder on the "Up field" side of him. He wraps his arms around him, goes to the ground and spins the ball carrier violently to the ground and out of bounds. I have no question that several concussions followed this drill.

Grass Drills: These are also called "Up Downs." Here each player runs in place and hits the ground at the whistle. He bounces up immediately and continues to run in place waiting for the next whistle. This drill was also used to gain the teams attention and for punishment for misbehavior.

Higher levels of conditioning were achieved by running "Gassers." This was an exercise engaged in by Don Shula of the Miami Dolphins. The team would run across the field and back two times. We did each set of these four times which basically gave us sixteen 50-yard sprints. And true to its title, we were gassed.

I would come home from those morning practices, eat a sandwich or two, then head for the cool of the basement for a nap. I slept for an hour or so, and then my mother would wake me up to head back to the school for our afternoon practice. As each day went by, I could feel the soreness leaving being replaced by greater levels of fitness.

But I would have to say, that the aspect of football that I came to enjoy most was being part of a team. Because some of the guys were new in town, and some came in from St. Margaret's, I got to know guys I hadn't met before and developed friendships around the game of football. I grew to appreciate everyone's commitment to hard work, sacrifice, and discipline.

My admiration and appreciation for one player came in one day. A few of the varsity players had been drinking over the weekend. Somehow, word got back to the coaches and after practice, discipline was administered to those who would admit it. A few of the players stood up and were directed to the side-lines for extra sprints. The rest of us were ordered off the field to watch the violators run. I watched our freshman quarterback stand up and go with the group. He ran with all the others but somehow, I felt that something was wrong. On the way back to the locker room, I asked him about it. He told me that he had been to a wedding that weekend and had a sip of wine during the reception. That day I saw honesty exemplified.

From Coach Dyer we learned phrases like: "Talk is cheap except on the telephone" and "Fatigue makes cowards of us all." During my senior year we scrimmaged Bronxville. We did really well which led Coach to enter the bus and exclaim, "Hey gang! We got us a wagon!" I don't think any of us knew what that meant other than it was something good. We also learned football philosophy built around the idea that, "If they don't score, we don't lose." Coach Dyer made the claim that baseball was his favorite sport, but football was his religion.

As a freshman, I was small, slow and couldn't catch a ball. But somehow, I became the tight end on the freshman team. I'm really not sure I made any contribution, and I don't think we won a game. The only pass thrown to me was a screen and I dropped it.

After football ended that freshman year, I went out for winter track. In those days there were very few indoor venues, so it was never referred to as "Indoor Track." The winters were extremely cold, but we learned that after the first mile or so, our bodies heated up to a comfortable level. We wore insulated tops and bottoms and covered them with shorts and a T-shirt. Gloves and a hat completed our gear. On a few occasions we would insulate our faces with Vaseline just to build a barrier between our skin and the bitter wind. It was not uncommon to finish a run and notice that our bangs were frozen solid.

Between all the running and puberty, I got fast. The next year I became a JV running back in the "Wishbone T-Triple option attack." Coach Joe Ryan was very demanding and expected total effort all the time. You went *all out*, or you were left out. When we would run sprints, I always ran hard and tried to cross the line first. This was a new experience for me. It wasn't so much that I had this great work ethic, I think it was more the enjoyment of winning.

That's also where I learned that speed without direction can end up in disaster. Outside of football, we might say that enthusiasm without vision leads to destruction.

As junior varsity players, we were on the soccer practice field doing a drill with the defense. They were lined up on one side of the sled and the backfield was lined up on the other side. Like the name implies, the seven-man sled is a long metal sled with upright panels holding pads. A player would fire out from the down position and hit the pad with his shoulder or hands. In this drill, the quarterback snapped the ball and the running backs sprinted toward the sideline to receive the pitch. The defense would fire out, hit the sled, and pursue the ball carrier after he caught the ball.

When the running back got the ball, he ran through the net-less soccer goal and made the defense work in tagging him. Everything was done at full speed. All went well until one particular sequence. The ball was snapped, I took my lead step and ran as hard as I could, looking for the pitch. Everything seemed to go in slow motion. I watched the ball leave the quarterback's hands and turn over and over as it came my way. The ball came to me, I caught it and took one step before running as hard as I could into the goal post. As you may surmise, I fumbled. The phrase "speed kills' went through my mind.

I broke my cup (which I was immeasurably thankful I was wearing), bent my face mask (they were metal covered in rubber), and developed a long bruise on my chest. Without a doubt, I didn't know what hit me! I felt like I'd been run over by the proverbial Mac truck. I remember Coach Ryan coming over to me as I lay on the ground doing a silent body check. He leaned over me and asked, "You okay?" When I gave him an unsure "Yes" he said, "Think of that as a good hit!" When I rose to lean on my elbow, the team fell on the ground in laughter. I wanted to join in the laughter, but somehow nothing seemed funny at that moment.

During my sophomore year, the varsity team lost a game they should have won. Coach Dyer announced to the team on Monday that he was so upset that he sat on his toilet and cried for an hour. He woke up the next day to find a toilet bowl perched on his front steps quietly placed there by the characters that ran up and down the fields of Pearl River high school.

I'll never forget the last day of football my junior year. By finishing the season, I had earned my varsity letter. This meant that I could buy and wear the varsity blue and white. I didn't have much money, so I bought my jacket from a senior named Sal. The jacket cost me $25 but to me it was priceless. With a needle and thread, my mother changed the five into a six and I ignored the number and position (FB) on the sleeve. I proudly wore my white leather sleeved jacket with the class number seventy-six on the back, every chance I could regardless of warmer weather.

My Pirate pride came out one evening as I was walking our dog Red and talking to our neighbor Marion. Around the corner came a car with a guy hanging out the window. He had a can of shaving cream and he sprayed me across the sleeve and front of my jacket—my letterman's jacket! Reacting quicker than I was thinking I picked up a rock and popped their car before they hit the gas. The car came to a screeching halt and the dog and I hit the woods across the street. They drove past a couple of times, and I hit them with a small rock each time from the cover of the woods. I circled around through a trail in the woods and crossed the street when they were out of sight. I knew they'd be back. Now it was time to have some fun—at their expense.

Moments later I had the window open and the curtain down in our room upstairs. With the lights off, I could lean out the window with my BB gun and plink them every time they went by. And that's what I did. I must have shot them four times as they came by. They couldn't tell which side of the road it came from so each time they stopped the car, jumped out and raced into the woods.

I was watching them turn around yet again and preparing for another shot when on came the lights to our room. There I was, a silhouette hanging out the window with my method of revenge extended. It was Casey! "Hey man! What's up?" I hollered for him to shut the lights off and then allowed him to enjoy my exercise in justice.

A few nights later Billy was at the house. He and Casey were upstairs, and I was in the den watching television. Billy came down and signaled for me to follow him. When I got to our room, Casey was on the bed. He said, "I think I'm gonna be sick!" He explained that he and Billy had been shooting random cars out the window. They shot a few enjoying the confusion of the drivers, when "Bam!" the side window of a car exploded.

We hid the gun, put the curtain back up, and did our best to act innocent. I'm certain I did a better job than Casey because I was in fact, innocent, at least on that night.

I have so many great memories of high school football. The camaraderie, the hard work, the winning (5-3-1 our senior year). All our athletic teams did well because we were committed to working hard and pushing each other to be our best. During the summer, my friend Chris who was a linebacker and I worked out together. We made a trail in the woods and would work on our quickness and agility by running the trail repeatedly.

Coach Dyer gave us lots of speeches meant to inspire us, but we were so young mentally that they mostly served to confuse us and give us things to laugh about later. "What are the last four letters in American? I can!" At halftime of the game against Clarkstown North (we were losing), we were given the history lesson about The Battle of Corregidor. The lesson started with him telling us that we didn't look like Americans. He told us, "You look like Japanese." The humor in this is found in the fact that our bus driver, who was in the gym with us, was himself Japanese. I'm not certain how he received this motivational speech. We were told that the American forces were pinned down with very limited ammunition and facing several thousand advancing Japanese soldiers. On our way back to the field a wide receiver leaned over to me and let me know that he was pretty sure that we lost that battle. Ironically, we went out on the field and lost that game as well.

When the season was over during our sophomore year, an upperclassman named Ray developed an entire league to play during the winter. It was called the "WFL." That stood for Winter Football League. It was complete with captains, a list of players to draft, and a full schedule. It was played in the snow and frozen ground and was full contact with no protective equipment. The coaches didn't know about it otherwise they would have shut it down.

One day, at the end of the one of our W.F.L. games, Mr. Lesko, who lived at the edge of the upper field came up to us and asked us for help. He was cutting a tree down and wanted us to pull the rope. We agreed and joined him in his back yard. I took one look at the large tree and had some real hesitations. I was working in my brother's tree service and was well seasoned in the task.

I immediately saw several problems. The tree was large and tall, and Mr. Lesko had put a rope up as far as his ladder would allow—

and it was not very high. At the base of the tree, he had cut pieces out as deep as his chainsaw could reach. The wind was blowing straight at the house. Nothing about the situation gave us confidence that this would end well.

As he made his last cut, the tree began to pull us toward the house. We pulled with all we had but were losing the battle. As the tree went toward the house it made a slight change of direction and fell with a violent crash across the above-ground pool. We stood there in silence and watched the tidal wave come across the trunk. Without a word, Mr. Lesko dropped the chainsaw and we turned and walked up the hill and back to the field.

When we got to the top and out of sight and earshot, we hit the ground laughing. All it took was for one of the guys to bring to our remembrance that Mr. Lesko had told us that he wanted to cut the tree down because the roots were growing under the pool and making bumps in the liner. Problem solved. No tree, no roots, no pool!

As a freshman, following winter track, I went out for the spring track team. I was a pole vaulter and did whatever else my coach told me to. Think about the vault: You're directed to take a long and flexible stick, run as fast as you can and plant it in a hole in the ground while holding it. Then bend it as much as you can as it lifts you off the ground. Rotate upside down and go as high as you can then land on your back. You don't have to be crazy to be a pole vaulter, but it will help.

I remember how I got started in pole vaulting. During the summer between 7th and 8th grade, my mother was setting up for a banquet in the high school cafeteria. After moving tables for her, I got bored and wandered down to the track. My friend and classmate Teddy was there pole vaulting. I talked to him and gave it a try. I cleared 7'6" before I headed back up to the school. Through that one exposure I was hooked. I went out for track that spring and pole vaulted, high jumped, and ran the hurdles. But the vault is where I found my home. My Dad taught me to bend the pole and as a freshman I cleared 10 feet. The next year I cleared 11' 6." During my Junior year I eclipsed 13'6" and by senior year I had surpassed the 14'3" mark. Winning came readily and I became All-State and launched a successfully competitive college career.

The pole vault lends itself to long competitions. One invitational meet I was in went so long, they had to put cars on the grass so we could see by the headlights. At another meet, I had to travel back home on another team's bus because our team was done while they had a vaulter left in the competition.

Unlike other sports and events, vaulters get a chance to make good friends during the long hours of competition. One of my friends was from Tappan Zee high school named Lance. He was a great athlete and held the state record in the vault. On more than one occasion someone would come into the cafeteria and let me know that Lance was outside and looking for me. Before long, he and I had strapped my pole on the outside of his Nova and were heading up the Palisades Parkway on our way to practice in the field house at West Point. We always found an open door to the field house and could get a couple of hours in before the custodian kicked us out. I have no doubt that he knew we weren't cadets, but I think he didn't see any harm in letting us have the run of the place for a little while.

Two other friends that I grew close to were from Suffern High School and were both named George. One of them had a vaulting pit in his back yard and he let me come over and practice any time I wanted. His runway was elevated and made of plywood. The surface was made from a synthetic rubber that he proudly lifted from the soon-to-be refurbished track at his school, Manhattan College which oddly enough, is located in the Bronx.

We were all fiercely competitive, but we never let our desire to win affect our friendship. We helped each other by catching poles, moving standard, offering advice, and sharing humor. We also helped each other by challenging and pushing one another to do our best. We were friends and it didn't matter if it was Saturday morning or Friday night.

Mom and Dad were never the kind of parents who manipulated us into sports. They never demanded playing time or special consideration for any of us. They let us participate in whatever we wanted and stayed in the background cheering us on. We were in the huddle in the middle of a football game. Just before Phil called the play, I unmistakably heard my mother's voice over everyone else's. "C'mon you Buccaneers!" I looked across and saw Wally and Mark with a look on their faces that said, "Was that your mother?" "Yup! That was my Mom!"

Something happened a couple of times during track practice that encapsulates the support I felt from my parents. The track and football field were in a bowl on the eastern edge of the school property. This means that the sun set in the direction of the school buildings. A couple of times, particularly my Senior year, while pole vaulting, I would look up on the hill, and with the sun setting in the west, see the silhouette of my father on the hill. Because of the sun, I couldn't make out any of his features, but I knew his shape. He didn't come down to the track, he just stayed on the hill, waved at me and watched us practice. It was moments like that when I felt the love and support that every son or daughter longs for.

My high school track coach was Coach Tom Doherty and he had a unique voice as well as a unique style. He was easy going but direct. You knew he cared, and you wanted to do well to impress and please him. He turned the entire track and cross-country programs around. In my freshman year we amassed a record of 0-10. We couldn't beat the track team from the school of the blind and lame. But by my senior year, we were 10-0 and simply couldn't be beaten by anyone. After I graduated, I talked to an older coach from a competing school, who watched the Pirate track team develop. He said they used to get ready for a meet against PR by asking the athletes what events they wanted to compete in. Then it transitioned into the coaches getting together to see what strategy they needed to try to hang in there with the Pirates. After college, I had the privilege of coaching with Tom Doherty for a couple of years and remain close friends with him today.

During my senior year I became the brunt of a joke perpetrated by the coaching staff. I'm not sure what their motivation was. Perhaps it was to break the tension that was building around the championship meets. Maybe they felt I needed to be taken down a notch or two. Possibly, it was because they were a bunch of characters and just wanted to enjoy a good laugh at my expense.

But for whatever reason, as I walked past the trophy case between the cafeteria and the gym, I noticed a big poster in the trophy case. There was my picture from second grade (which means my mother was in on it too) with the words surrounding it reading:

"CONGRATULATIONS TO STEVE JIRGAL—REGIONAL WINNER OF THE HOWDIE DOODY LOOK-ALIKE CONTEST. STEVE WILL BE COMPETING IN THE NATIONAL COMPETITION IN PROV UTAH!"

What do you do with that? Ignore it? Find a way to get rid of it? Or relax and enjoy a few laughs on yourself? I chose to do the latter. Several kids pointed it out with hopes of embarrassing me. I just rolled with the punches. I explained to them that I won a T.V., stereo, and $500 cash. I told them that I would be traveling to Utah in July and might win a car if I came in first. Their jeers quickly turned to jealousy.

I had forgotten to correct that information before the noise died down and all was forgotten. But during my Freshman year of college, at a New Year's Eve party my buddy Wayne came up and asked me how the competition had gone. It took a few minutes to convince him that it was all a joke and that there was no competition and no prizes.

As I said before, my entire high school experience was so much fun. Most of this is due to the characters we had in our class. We had great athletes but also had a bunch of kids with amazing senses of humor. I've learned that each year of school brings with it emotions and energies:

Freshman year: Fear. You don't know most of the other students and you avoided the older ones for fear of getting bullied. More than a few freshmen were pulled into the bathroom and given a twirly top. This is done by lifting the helpless boy up and dipping his hair in the swirling water of a toilet.

Freshmen were also the target of practical jokes. One of the jokes was to put a funnel in the top of your pants and a quarter on your forehead as you held your head back. The idea was to move your head forward to cause the quarter to slip off your forehead and into the funnel in your pants. It was demonstrated by an upper classman, but when the freshman was in position with his head back and quarter in place, an arm came from the crowd and poured a carton of milk in the funnel causing a clearly visible and souring stain.

Sophomore year: Seeking. Sophomores are committed to finding a group or niche to fit in. Athletics, band, academics, drugs, and the performing arts are some of the categories tenth graders look to segue way in to. Everyone is seeking to fit in somewhere and quite often students bounce from group to group until they reach a place of acceptance. Unfortunately, some wind up in a destructive group and others never seem to find their place.

Junior year: Jockeying. Everyone seems to be jockeying to find their place of significance. This is where prom queens (and today, prom kings) are chosen and sometimes varsity team captains are selected. Class rank comes into focus with thoughts of college entrance becoming more significant.

Senior year: Swagger. Seniors have learned the system and have a clear idea of what's expected of them and what they can get away with. They know their way around and understand that they are at the top of the food chain. They rule the school! Certain classes can be skipped, and others can be ignored (even when attended). Senior cut day is heavily participated in with groups running to the beach, friend's houses, and Bear Mountain.

My Senior Swagger showed itself in many ways. I had a nickname for the principal of the school. His name was Mr. Riker. I called him "Warden Riker." I wasn't shy about it and would yell to him down the hall. He even signed my yearbook hoping that someday I would vault high enough to make it "Over the wall."

I got kicked out of the library a record number of times due to talking and called several of my teachers by their first names. I cut classes regularly when I knew there would be no consequences and often made myself at home in the teacher's lounge.

I spent a good bit of time in the library. I did very little studying there. I just saw it as a good place to go and hang out with a group of friends. Diane, Mary Grace, Dave, John, Cathy, Tom, and a host of others could always be found in this *hang out* place of higher learning.

One day Billy thought it would be a good idea to make a copy of his face in the library copier. We didn't think much of it until we saw what he was doing. He stuck his face on the glass and pushed the button. When the light came on, he realized that it might have been a good idea to close his eyes. He staggered back to our table dazed with his eyes blinking and watering. Our sympathy lights never came on.

Back in those days everyone's jeans were notoriously tight. It almost looked like they were painted on. You could almost tell the date on a dime in someone's back pocket. One day while heading up the stairs from the cafeteria with a few friends, Steve, who somehow had his hands in his front pockets tripped over a step. He fell against the wall and fought with everything he had to get his hands free. He slowly slid down the wall and lay on his stomach on the stairs. We didn't even step toward him to help. In fact, he may be in that stairwell today.

The girls were real characters as well. Some of them even more so than the boys. One day in chemistry class, Beth passed out in the back of the room. Mr. Stanley came to her aid. He was taking her pulse and asking her questions before deciding whether to call 911. While he was doing that Bobby was at the front desk adjusting several students' test marks. Beth experienced a quick and full recovery and many of us (including me) did better than expected as far as grades were concerned.

On Friday nights the gym at the high school was open for free play and hanging out. When the location of the high school was downtown the same concept was exercised but was called *The Pirate's Hideaway*. Most of the inside activity involved basketball and weightlifting while the outside activity included everything from drinking and dancing to street fighting. On many occasions when the gym would close for the night, we would head to Rex's Pizza in a nearby town or wander down to the bleachers at the football field to begin a "Bleacher Party." Someone brought beer and as many as fifty kids would gather to continue their Friday night activities. Usually, the music got loud enough for a nearby resident to complain and the police would arrive to break things up.

On one night two police cars arrived to shut things down. The group of students made their way back toward the gym and merged with the group hanging out there. The police tried to break that group up as well and nudged them up the hill. In the shadows of the hill is where the "Heads" hung out together to get high. Now the group of students was well over one hundred and the numbers gave us great confidence. Though I didn't want to miss the action, I saw what was developing and was smart enough to stay in the back of the crowd out of harm's way.

Over the loudspeakers we were told to disperse but refused. Several more police cars showed up and we were again told to leave the property. None of us moved. The police shined their lights on us and that's when the rock began to be thrown. The cars were hit, and the lights were smashed. The police tried to grab several students, but they all seemed to get away. Somehow the entire crowd moved its way up to the parking lot of the nearby grocery store.

In the parking lot, one student named Tommy became increasingly belligerent. He was bold enough to confront a nearby cop. I heard the cop ask him, "Do you want to get arrested?" He leaned forward and screamed, "I'm underage! Ha Ha!" He was wrong! In seconds he was on his belly and cuffed. They lifted him into the back seat of the car and went back to confronting the rest of the crowd. We all howled and cheered when we saw Tommy get out of the car and begin running across the parking lot. He was caught after a short chase and put back in the car. I've often wondered what would have happened if he got away. How do you explain away hand cuffs to your parents? Looking back, that was a night that I was not too proud of us as PR Pirates.

One morning during breakfast, Casey who was looking over the T.V guide, informed me that "The Night of the Living Dead" would be on television that night. This was a movie that introduced the world to zombies and the darker types of movies. We had heard so much about it from our friends but had never seen it ourselves. We agreed that we would watch it together that night.

I got wrapped up in my usual routine on Friday night and found myself at open gym. I had forgotten all about the movie. After everything closed, I made my way home. When I opened the front door, I heard Casey's voice come from the den, "Who came in?" In a moment I realized he was watching "The Night of the Living Dead." I yelled and jumped into the room startling my brother. He was sitting in a chair with his hair matted against his forehead with sweat.

I watched the movie with him grabbing him every once in a while, and receiving a punch on the arm for my efforts. The movie ended and the danger began for me. My job was to walk the dog each night before bed. This meant that I had to be outside by the woods where the Ghouls waited for me to arrive.

That night, the dog set a record in how slow he could finish his business. My senses were elevated. every falling leaf, snap of a twig, or cry of a bird set me on edge. The dog finally finished, and we hurried back to the safety of the house.

At the front steps I got an idea which I don't claim to be good with any level of consistency. It tied the dog to the railing and climbed up the front of the house. I walked along the short roof to the window of the room Casey and I shared. The head of the beds were at the wall where the window was, and the curtains were parted about a foot. The lamp on the nightstand was on and I pressed my face against the glass just above it. In the bathroom mirror, I could see Casey brushing his teeth.

The ultimate fear prank was about to take place. Casey entered the room and walked directly toward the window. He didn't see me at first but when he did, all the color fled from his face. He froze and locked his eyes on me. Then recognition came to him, and I watched him collapse on the bed. It was a night I've never forgotten.

Reflecting on that night, I'm just glad the police didn't show up and find me on the roof. I have no doubt that Casey would have denied knowing me and would be beside himself in laughter as they took me away for the attempted breaking and entering.

Halfway through our senior year I began to date Diane. She was a pretty girl with a winning smile and plenty of friends. She played tennis and was a majorette. We went to parties, canoed, hit the movies, cruised, and hung out with friends. On Friday nights I would hang out with my buddies at open gym while Diane worked the fitting room at Bamberger's in the Nanuet Mall. When she finished work, I would pick her up and we would go to a party or cruise around for a couple of hours. She went to college in New York while I headed off to Gettysburg, Pa. We continued to date until halfway through our sophomore years when we parted ways.

As Seniors, Wally and I were together in every class except homeroom. Wally had a great sense of humor and it seemed like we laughed the entire day. Phys. Ed. was the pivotal point of our humor. Mr. Ed Bowden was the teacher of senior physical education, and we had a great time with him. Because of our senior swagger, we knew we could get away with calling him Phys. Ed. That year, the entire semester was centered around "Lifetime Sports." We participated in tennis, badminton, square dancing, archery, golf, softball, and a few other sports. During golf, Wally and I slipped out of class with a couple of clubs and drew our own course throughout the school. We interrupted classes with a request to "Play through" as we hit each teacher's desk with a ball.

There was a giant curtain suspended from the ceiling that divided the gym in two. The climbing rope was right at the edge of the curtain. Each day during archery class, with my bow across my chest, I would pull the rope around the curtain and wait for Phys. Ed to call the roll. When he came to my name, on cue, I swung on the rope (remember I was a pole vaulter), over the entire class and dropped down in front of everyone. I saluted the group and called out, "Welcome to Sherwood!" This brought laughter from some and a shaking of the head from others.

When the weather got warm it simply meant that Wally and I added swimming to the curriculum. Our school didn't have a pool, but Laurie did! Her family lived on the edge of the athletic fields. So, donning our shorts and with a towel over our shoulders we headed to her house for a swim. Again, part of the senior swagger.

I was never much of a drinker. I went to all the parties and enjoyed time with my friends, but I had convictions that kept me from imbibing. But it almost seemed like a law that when you became eighteen (the legal drinking age then) you were obligated to sit at the bar and have at least one drink with a buddy.

I turned eighteen during December of my senior year. My buddy Mike came by on Friday night with plans of helping me fulfill my obligation. He was my *designated driver* (and he was already eighteen) and we set out to hit all the hot spots. He bought me my first drink, but I carried enough money to foot my indulgences the rest of the night. To say that I overdid it would be an understatement. We hit *The Triangle, The Black Bull Pub, Grasshoppers*, and I'm sure a few other places that I don't remember due to the places I do recall. I do remember decorating the men's room in colors they had not chosen. I also remember meeting Coach D'Agostino in a convenient store and somehow having a conversation with him. I have no recollection of going home but I'm sure that I did. The next morning, I had track practice and it is no surprise that it was one of my least enjoyable days on the planet.

Because I was a pole vaulter it was easy to spend a good bit of time recovering on the mat. I'm not sure I even took one jump that day. Whether or not Coach Doherty was wise to what was going on, I'll never know.

Coach Max Talaska was our Athletic Director. He was a great guy with a deep voice and strong arms, and I always felt like I was one of his favorites. He was well into his senior years but always stayed in great shape. One day as I was passing him in the gym, he reached out and grabbed me. We got into a sort of wrestling hold, and he had all of my attention. I was so surprised at how strong a man he was, and I was thankful he didn't put a move on me that I'm sure would have had me quickly and embarrassingly on my back.

Wrestling was a dominant sport in New York. At P.R. thanks to the work of Coach Larry Ruderman in the middle school, and Coaches Julius D'Agostino Hayes Yorks and Tom Lanks in the high school, we were always contenders for the county championship. The matches themselves were held in the gym but the team had their own wrestling room complete with wall-to-wall mats and a sign on the ceiling that read, "If you can read this, you are pinned."

There was an elite club within the fraternity of wrestlers. These were special wrestlers called "BAGUBAs" This stood for "**B**rutally **A**ggressive **G**uy **U**ninhibited **B**y **A**dversity." If you ever saw a Pirate with a T-shirt that said BAGUBA you knew you were in the company of greatness. The only thing that a BAGUBA feared was another BAGUBA!

Before the advances of medicine and the rules prohibiting it, guys would cut an amazing amount of weight to wrestle in a lower weight class. Most of the time this was attained through the practice of dehydration, and it was very common for one of these athletes to cut class and hit the road with a plastic suit on.

There were some matches that were going to be so strongly contested that if you didn't get there early enough, you weren't admitted due to fire code violations. Kids were everywhere and often had to sit on the floor on the edge of the mat. On more than one occasion, someone would be kicked or landed on by the two grapplers.

When the team came out to warm up, each of the wrestlers would bang the door against the wall making a rhythmic bang as he entered the gym. The crowd went crazy and one's ears were ringing for an hour after leaving the gym.

Because our team was so good, the wrestlers participated in *Pin Pools*. Each of the guys on the team pitched in a dollar and the pool of money was held by the manager. The wrestler that had the quickest pin was given the treasure.

One of my favorite coaches was Coach Hayes Yorks. His nickname was "Purp" or "Purple Violet Hayes." He taught physics and coached football, wrestling, softball, little league, and anything else he was asked to coach. He was a gentle giant standing over six-foot-four and weighing well over 300 pounds. He was easy to talk to and quick with a joke or story. His heart was clearly as big as his body.

In the current educational landscape, it is unheard of for a student to be disciplined by paddling. But in those bygone days it wasn't a rarity for a student to be stood up and wacked with a wooden implement. In a strange way, some even saw it as a badge of honor to be struck during class. The number of swings and the force of the blows corresponded to the violation. In my younger days, if our parents learned that you got hit once in school, you could count on a second pop at home. It always seemed to be *guilty as charged*.

As was mentioned earlier, Hayes Yorks was very easy going. But he was a paddler. His paddle rested against the wall behind his desk and was aptly used in extreme cases.

In the gym one day, while strapping the front of the vaulting mats together, I had a sense that the ground was shaking. I looked up just in time to see "Purp" airborne and heading straight for my chest. I ducked just in time, and he went flying over me and landed in the center of the mat. My life flashed before my eyes, and I was brought back to reality with his deep and infectious laughter.

Just outside the library I came across a circle of students with two in the middle ready to square off with each other. No one was stopping them. Everyone was there to see a good show and breathe a breath of gratitude that they were not in the center of the circle. Just before the first punch was thrown, I heard the booming voice of Hayes Yorks. "I get the winner!" was all he said. The two boys looked at his massive size and the violent episode was put to rest.

Driving in cars with no destination in mind was just a part of life. Mom always let me borrow her car when she wasn't going anywhere so I enjoyed plenty of motorized freedom. But a truth I've found is that if you're a character on two feet, you'll be a character with one of those feet on the gas pedal. Some of the guys had their own cars and it wasn't hard to jump in and wheel away the night. Others like myself, had to borrow from family members.

Billy was one who had to borrow a car. I watched him with masterful technique wear his sister down so he could borrow her Maverick. He made every kind of promise known to man (none of which he kept) until finally she caved and threw the keys at him. Then we were off to who knows where and to do who knows what. I honestly didn't know if we would live or die that night. The only thing I was sure is there would be danger and laughter on the road ahead.

Spontaneity was the rule and nothing we did was scripted or prompted. It was just a "Drive by the seat of your pants" experience. On a Saturday afternoon we found ourselves gliding down Holt Avenue. A lady was in her yard when Billy pulled up to the curb.

Billy: "Excuse me Ma'am. Do you know where Walker Street is?"
Lady: "No. I'm sorry but I don't think I do."
Billy: "Okay. Listen up. You go down to the end of the block and turn right. Then you go two blocks and turn right again. Walker street will be on your left."
Lady (very confused): "Oh. Okay. Thanks!"
Billy: "No problem. Have a good day!"
Lady: "You too!"

And then two knuckleheads would drive away holding their laughter for fifty yards.

While in my dad's station wagon, I met up with Billy and Wally at Mr. Softy's. It was a local ice cream hangout on Middletown Road. We talked for a while and before long found ourselves racing on Route 304. Billy was in his sister's Maverick-a six cylinder, while I had my dad's wagon, an eight cylinder. It wasn't much of a contest, but I had to make a statement, so I cranked that old boy up to 103 miles per hour. I'm certain that's the fastest Dad's car had gone in the history of its life. I'll never know since I didn't want to tip my hand by asking him.

After pre-season football practice one Saturday afternoon a pile of guys got into Billy's sister's Maverick for the ride home. When we got to Don's house it was clear that Billy had been there multiple times before. There were several pairs of *burn out* marks in front of the house. Don jumped out of the back seat, but Billy was stopped by Don's mother quickly moving toward the car.

"Billy! Billy! Now you just wait a minute!"
"Yes Ma'am!"
"Look at this road! Look at these marks here. You did this!"
"Yes M'aam!"
"I don't want you patching out in front of our house any-more. Do you understand me?"
"Yes Ma'am!"

With that she walked away. Billy didn't say anything immediately, but I knew the mental wheels were turning. He looked over at me with the smile of a person who knew the punchline to the world's greatest joke. He began to rev the engine.

"No" I said, "You're not gonna..."

I never got to complete the sentence.

With a belch, a cloud of smoke, and an echoing screech the car slid forward, and we were gone from sight.

Intersecting with Middletown Road is Crooked Hill Road. The name is appropriate. This road is long and carries with it several twists and turns. At one of these turns was a house with a large tree on the front end of the property. Late one night, Billy and I drove to this turn and for some reason Billy pulled the car almost onto the yard, and very close to the tree. I had no idea what he was up to, but based on experience, I knew I would find out soon enough.

He put the car in reverse and hit the gas leaving a pair of marks back out onto the street. Then he pulled back up to the tree and instructed me, "Now let's lay down and pretend we're dead!" That was over the edge and for some reason he couldn't understand why I opted out of that one. There is truth to the adjusted adage: You can take the boy out of the streets, but you can't take the streets out of the boy.

We had a witch who lived at the edge of town between Pearl River and Montvale. We had several old ladies who could easily be labeled witches, but we had a real bonified practicing witch whose name oddly enough, was Hazel. The Journal News carried an article on her, and it was framed and placed on the wall of the Nanuet Restaurant where she worked as a waitress. It showed her house (which looked haunted) and her room full of candles and her bed which was a coffin. She waited on some of us several times and although we were somewhat cautious, no event occurred to give us rise.

But that didn't stop us from visiting her house on a Friday night. We stood on her front lawn and yelled for her to come out. To heighten the humor, Mark climbed up on her porch and raised a chair at us. We ran away. Not because of Mark and the chair, but because Hazel had come out on the porch and was standing behind Mark with her arms folded. As I looked over my shoulder, I saw him jump the railing and head for the car. When we got to the car, the police were waiting. Thankfully all we got was a lecture and a warning and we were strongly advised to find something else to do.

Rockland cemetery was more than a place to bury the dead. During our Senior year we learned that it was also a place to bury our boredom. The cemetery is nestled in the woods on the eastern edge of Orangetown along a mountain ridge called Clausland Mountain. The top of the ridge overlooks the majestic Hudson River and is occupied by a multitude of grave sites along with a mausoleum. The road up to the top is almost a half-mile and is dotted with many grassy areas housing numerous grave sites. So, as you travel along the paved road to the top you pass several small grave sites on your way to the large one at the top. I had always heard the fanciful stories about this place but had never been there myself. So, when some of the guys suggested we pay the place a visit on Friday night before a party, I was all in.

But when Friday rolled around, we learned that several of the usual hang-out guys couldn't go. Chris had to watch his sister. Mark had to help his dad at home. John had to work. Nevertheless, we were determined to follow through with our plan to discover the scariest side of the county.

I rode with Billy, Wayne, and Wally. When we passed the gate and drove by the large field at the bottom, our anxiety began to rise. Nothing but darkness engulfed us, and the air was completely still.

We slowly worked our way up the hill and came to a large branch lying across the road. None of us wanted to get out and move it for fear of being left among the dead but together we exited the car, grabbed the large branch, tossed it aside, and raced back to the car. Secure inside, we continued our climb to the top. When we came around a turn and down a slope, our headlights brightened the sight of a ghost hanging from a tree.

It was a very amateur rendition of a ghost, but it grabbed our attention. It was simply made with a sheet taped to a Clorox bottle with eyes and a mouth made of electrical tape. None of us admitted that we were startled but the collective inhalation in the car told us all otherwise.

We maneuvered around the *point of horror* and worked our way further toward the mausoleum. At the top of the ridge there is a large circle going around the mass of graves. The mausoleum is found on the far ride side of the circle. We sat for just a moment at the intersection of the pavement when we heard a loud pop. We turned and saw a ghost running from one gravestone and disappear behind another. Our laughter was interrupted by another blast and the sight of another ghost running for cover.

At that point we knew who these harbingers of death were. It was Chris, Mark, and John, our buddies who had other "Responsibilities" and couldn't make it. We got out of the car, called them by name and enjoyed a few laughs.

We dismissed to the previously planned party at Steve's house and found it to be in full swing. For some reason, Steve's father felt it was acceptable to provide beer for all of Steve's guests (and there were a bunch of us) and our underaged minds agreed with his decision.

Of course, our previous adventure was a hot topic at the party. For some reason that I still don't understand, I made the comment that the cemetery was really not that scary. This started a discussion followed by a series of dares. Before I knew it, most of the party were in cars and headed out to the aforementioned source of some level of anxiety.

The motivation to follow the dare was monetary. Money was collected at the party and the prize (about $20) was mine if I would walk to the top and back. When the crowd arrived at the entrance to the cemetery, I was driven to the top so I would be familiar with the road. A lanyard was placed on the door handle of the mausoleum and my assignment was to walk up the road, retrieve the evidence of a completed mission, and walk back and collect my well-earned reward.

When I left the row of cars, music was playing, people were drinking, dancing, and celebrating. Through a firm but somewhat nervous voice, I had given strict instructions that no one was to jump out at me from any of the naturally dark hiding places. The promise of violence was used to punctuate my threat.

I quickly worked my way up the road and in short order had the lanyard around my neck and was making my way back down to the crowd. When I came out of the woods, I was met by car horns, flashing lights, and cheering. I collected the money and tried my best to convince the group that there was nothing to be afraid of.

Don sided with me and agreed to walk up alone. His only hesitation was that he would be stranded by his friends. So, Billy gave him his house key as a bargaining chip and off he went. He was gone a very long time, much longer than I was gone and so it was concluded that he was lost. Except for three of us, everyone left and went back to the party. We drove up the mountain to find Don.

Two trips up the hill failed to find our friend. While we were sitting on the car's hood, and discussing what to do, out came Don from the woods. We asked him where he had been, and he tried to convince us that he was just out walking in the woods. The story was interrupted by the arrival of a squad car that blocked our escape.

We were questioned and ordered into the car for a drive through the grounds to assess if any damage had been done to any of the gravesites. Never having been in a police car before, I was excited and unintimidated and jumped into the front seat marveling at all the dials, switches, and wires. While riding along I heard whispers of *ghost* from the back seat and realized that we were about to come upon the ghost still hanging from the tree. When the lights from the police car hit it, the officer hit his brakes and shared with us a few of his "emergency words." I was told to get out and remove the object of fear. I pulled on the sheet and the head came off leaving me with nothing but fabric in my hand and a Clorox head bouncing and swinging from the branch.

Completing the trip and finding no damage we were driven to our car. The officer had already assessed that none of us could drive after 9 o'clock (New York State law), so we were taken to police headquarters. It was now after two in the morning. One of our parents was to be contacted for us to be picked up. That's when our fear set in.

For some reason, Billy's father was chosen possibly because he seemed to be the one who might be least upset by the phone call and the early morning trip to the police station. When he arrived, very little was said. He quietly instructed us to get in the car and we traveled silently back to our respective homes.

I was not overly concerned. I didn't have a curfew and our house was always unlocked—yes, even in New York. It was after 3 o'clock when I was dropped off and my confidence waned when I tried each door. The house was locked up solid. Around the back of the house, I found a ladder leading to the window in the bedroom that Casey and I shared.

While climbing the ladder, I looked in the window and saw my dad seated in a chair reading a book. It was not uncommon for my father to be up reading, so I didn't think much of it. I went downstairs to let him know that I was home and to relate to him the funny parts of the evening.

Dad was visibly amused and was enjoying the details of my story until I got to the part where the cops showed up. I knew immediately that I had to lighten the seriousness of the story, so I quickly threw my best rendition of Barney Fife. He relaxed and I concluded my time with him free of worry and on good terms.

The next day, as expected my mother enjoyed the story of the previous night's escapades. Ironically, both my parent's resting place is at the top of Rockland Cemetery. On several of my visit's home, I've been to visit their graves and each time I sit on their bench my mind flies back to the night that my friends and I spent there.

Each academic year the height of excitement was centered around the Senior trip to Washington, D.C. It was a Pearl River High School tradition. Because of the size of our class, five buses were needed to make the trip which took place over the Thanksgiving holiday. So many stories evolved making great conversation for the five-hour trip home, but little did I know that I would soon be providing subject matter for homeward conversations.

We had barely pulled away from the school when one of the young ladies informed me that she had a problem. She had strapped a bottle of vodka to her waist with an ace wrap. Somehow upon seating, the bottle broke spilling the vodka all over her. Fortunately, the clear liquid gives off little odor, so she didn't get caught.

When we arrived in D.C., we were given our room keys and sent in to settle down. I shared a room with Wayne, Tony, Teddy, and Mike. That first night, we had plans to sneak out and tour the town. Late that night, I opened the door to see if it was all clear. I looked one way and saw no one. I called to the guys and took a step out into the hall to head for the stairs. In a chair by the stairwell was Hayes Yorks, one of the chaperones smiling and holding the end of a fire hose pointed in our direction. We made a hasty retreat and gave up the idea of a night out. We did however call the front desk and report a man in the hall threatening people with the hose. We didn't go out but heard a muffled conversation between Hayes and a security guard.

We toured the White House, the zoo, the capitol, and the Smithsonian Institute. It was this last place that always comes to mind when I think about D.C. I bounced around with my buddies seeing everything we could see in the time that was allotted. This was to be our last stop before heading home.

As we were going up the escalator to the gem room, Mary and her friends were coming down. I called out to her and asked her what was in the room. She let me know that the *Hope Diamond* was housed up there. I told her that I was going to steal it and give it to her as an engagement ring without any idea that I was making a prophetic statement. She agreed to my offer.

We toured the room and came to the place where the *Hope Diamond* was. It was kept in a recessed case with thick glass covering it. Mark, John, and Chris stood next to me as we looked at the large diamond. A young boy asked, "I wonder how thick the glass is." Mark said, "If you bang your head against it you'll find out!" That gave me an idea. Maybe I could tap the glass and get an idea of its thickness. I tapped the glass. Then I tapped it a little harder. Finally, I popped it gently with my fist. That's when the alarm went off and the entire place was in a lock-down state.

Before I knew what happened, two guards had me and John against the wall and had our wallets out. We were rushed to the basement and placed in a holding cell. I couldn't believe this was happening. The officers were lecturing us and yelling alternatively. We were informed that there were agents all over the city racing toward the building.

We were momentarily relieved when Hayes Yorks showed up. My heart that was in my stomach returned to the proper place. He announced that he was there to "collect the boys" and was told, "Shut up fat man. These boys aren't going anywhere soon!" It was then that my heart rocketed into my throat. More berating followed and somehow Hayes convinced one of the officers to let us go.

The entire class was on the buses and were waiting to start the long trip home. When we left the building, John's bus was the first we came to. My bus, however, was at the front of the line. I had to walk past all the buses to get to it. It takes no imagination to understand the comments that were hurled from the windows of each bus. In laughing tones, I was asked "Where's Bonnie Clyde?" and "Hey Jirgal, do you still have the rock." More than one person yelled, "Hey man, I saw your picture in the post office!"

When my mother picked me up from the school, the first thing she asked me was, "So, how was your trip." My reply was, "Unbelievable. I'll tell you about it when I get home so I can tell Dad too." I was smart enough to know that I had to get to my parents before the school did.

When I was telling them all about the trip, I watched my father's face fall when I mentioned the Hope Diamond incident. I covered it quickly with a few points of humor and we got past it.

I know my parents were over it when I opened my stocking that Christmas. In the bottom of my stocking was a plastic case containing a large (fake) diamond ring. The note said, "I HOPE you can find a way to stay out of trouble." The entire family was staring at me waiting for my reaction. I stared at the ring and was completely silent. No words would come from my mouth. I have it on good authority that at that very moment, icicles could be seen hanging down from the ceiling of hell. When I smiled, the entire family burst out in laughter at my expense.

A CLOSING THOUGHT

It was never my intention to communicate that Pearl River was a perfect place in which to grow up. And it can easily be concluded that I was not a perfect child growing up there. But Pearl River was a wonderful place for me to grow up and I am blessed to believe that historically, this all happened at a really good time. Pearl River has been nicknamed *The Town of Friendly People* and I have found this to be true. Because my brothers and sisters still live there, I am drawn back to this hamlet and each time I visit, my mind is flooded with great memories of my days as a boy. The days filled with laughter, adventure, struggles, and friendships will forever come my mind bringing the satisfaction of a smile, fulfillment, and even laughter. I no longer live in Pearl River, but Pearl River will always live in me.

REFLECTIONS

A distant memory your mind does seek,
To part the waters of the muddy creek.
You search your thoughts of long ago,
When time revealed your friends to know.

You found that trees were meant for climbing,
And insulting words went deep with rhyming.
The dirt and grime were as naught to you,
When mixed with colors like white and blue.

You learned so much apart from school,
Of dangers, and joys, the golden rule.
With family all about the home,
It brought in courage to romp and roam.

With hopes and dreams and plans to make,
You turned aside adventures to take.
With thoughts of how to spend the day
You knew you'd have to make your way.

As time and friends would onward go,
You settled with yourself to know.
You never guessed how life would unfurl,
When you spent your youth inside the pearl.

And maybe someday when thoughts come your way,
And your life finally stops its restless whirl,
You'll count it a joy and be able to say,
You're blessed to have spent so much time in the Pearl.

ABOUT THE AUTHOR
DR. STEVEN A. JIRGAL

Dr. Jirgal is a 1980 graduate of Gettysburg College where he became a four-time conference champion, All-American, and inductee to the Middle Atlantic Conferecnce *All Century Team* in the pole vault. He holds an undergraduate degree in health education and physical education. Following graduation, he taught on the high school and college level while coaching football and track in both venues. He holds masters degrees in health education, sports medicine, and divinity, as well as a doctorate in ministry.

He has been the director of Sports Medicine at Wingate University, area director for the Fellowship of Christian Athletes and has served on the staff of Hickory Grove Baptist Church in Charlotte, NC, as well as leading Lakeview Baptist Church, in Monroe, NC and Anderson Grove Baptist Church as the Senior Pastor. He presently serves as the "Pastor to the Pastors" at Lee Park Church. He has served on the local board of directors for the Fellowship of Christian Athletes, the board of trustees at New Orleans Baptist Seminary and the ministerial board of Wingate University. He currently serves on the board of directors for The Carolina Study Center, and Fathers in Touch ministry.

Dr. Jirgal is the founder and director of *The Jirgal Leadership Institute* where he strives to equip people for success in leadership roles. He and his wife Pam have three children, Joshua, Caleb, and Sarah. They reside in Monroe, NC.

OTHER BOOKS BY DR. JIRGAL
(DESCRIPTIONS TO BE FOUND ON THE JIRGAL
LEADERSHIP WEBSITE AT JIRGALLEADERSHIP.COM)

The Path of a Champion
Dying to Live
Life Points
Laws to Live By
Principles of Wholeness
Running a Clean Race
Encounters with the Christ
The Going to Bed Book
Intentional Steps
52 Words
Mining the Mind of King Solomon
From the Pages of Qoheleth